Other "Four Views" Books:

THE MEANING OF THE MILLENNIUM *edited by Robert G. Clouse. Four theologians debate the major millennial views: historic premillennialism, dispensational premillennialism, postmillennialism and amillennialism.*

WAR *edited by Robert G. Clouse. Theologians and philosophers examine four approaches to war: nonresistance, pacifism, just war and preventive war.*

WOMEN IN MINISTRY *edited by Robert G. Clouse and Bonnidell Clouse (forthcoming—late 1986).*

PREDESTINATION & FREE WILL

Four Views of Divine Sovereignty & Human Freedom by

John Feinberg
Norman Geisler
Bruce Reichenbach
Clark Pinnock

**Edited by David Basinger &
Randall Basinger**

INTERVARSITY PRESS
DOWNERS GROVE, ILLINOIS 60515

InterVarsity Press is the book-publishing division of Inter-Varsity Christian Fellowship, a student movement active on campus at hundreds of universities, colleges and schools of nursing. For information about local and regional activities, write IVCF, 233 Langdon St., Madison, WI 53703.

Distributed in Canada through InterVarsity Press, 860 Denison St., Unit 3, Markham, Ontario L3R 4H1, Canada.

All biblical quotes, unless otherwise indicated, are from the Revised Standard Version of the Bible, copyrighted 1946, 1952 © 1971, 1973. Used by permission.

All biblical quotations marked NIV are from the Holy Bible, New International Version. Copyright © 1973, 1978, International Bible Society. Used by permission of Zondervan Bible Publishers.

Cover photograph: Michael Goss

ISBN 0-87784-567-0

Printed in the United States of America

Library of Congress Cataloging in Publication Data
Main entry under title:

Predestination and free will.

   Bibliography: p.
   1. Predestination—Addresses, essays, lectures.
2. God—Omnipotence—Addresses, essays, lectures.
3. Providence and government of God—Addresses, essays, lectures.
4. Freedom (Theology)—Addresses, essays, lectures.
5. Free will and determinism—Addresses, essays, lectures.
I. Basinger, David.   II. Basinger, Randall, 1950-
BT810.2.P74   1986   234'.9   85-23887
ISBN 0-87784-567-0

19	18	17	16	15	14	13	12	11	10	9	8	7	6	5	4	3	2
99	98	97	96	95	94	93	92	91	90	89	88	87	86				

In memory of our father, Emerson

Introduction

David Basinger
Randall Basinger

THE CHRISTIAN FAITH PRESENTS US WITH A DILEMMA. ON THE one hand, we believe that God made us morally responsible beings with the ability to make meaningful moral decisions. If we were not able to make meaningful decisions, then why would Scripture exhort us to turn from evil things or to lead godly lives? If we were not responsible for freely choosing our actions, then how could God justly reward or punish us for them?

On the other hand, Christians also believe that God has sovereign control over all earthly affairs. He is the Lord of history and the Lord of our lives. We go to bed each night with the assurance that everything that occurs fits into his all-encompassing, preordained plan. Nothing can thwart God's plan; all that occurs is in keeping with his will.

The dilemma becomes clear. Can both of these basic Christian beliefs be true? If we are really able to make meaningful moral decisions, then must we not be able to act against God's will? If this is so, then how can we maintain that all that occurs is in keeping with his will? If humans are free, how can God be sovereign? On the other hand, if God is in control, how can human choices be real? In what sense can we be held responsible for actions if God is responsible for everything? Can we be free and yet predestined?

The Practical Tension

This tension exists not only in theory but also in the practice of Christian discipleship. What we believe does (and should) affect how we live. How Christians view the relationship between divine sovereignty and human freedom has a direct bearing on how they respond to various issues in their lives. But living out our beliefs in relation to divine sovereignty and human freedom presents significant problems. While most Christians believe in *both* divine sovereignty and human freedom, when faced with real-life situations, we/they often tend to emphasize one to the exclusion of the other.

Take for example the nuclear disarmament debate. Some Christians urge us to speak out and take action against the arms build-up. If we do not act quickly and decisively, we are warned, a worldwide nuclear disaster is inevitable. The assumption here is clear: human choice and action make a difference. People are to some extent responsible for the destiny of the human race. On the other hand, some Christians, who are not convinced that working for nuclear disarmament is really appropriate, argue that God is sovereign over human history. Thus, as one evangelical has argued, "The fate of the earth doesn't rest on the whims or maneuverings of any man or nation, but in God's all-powerful hands. . . . His plan will prevail."[1]

On a less global level, take the missionary candidate who is having difficulty raising her support. She may believe God is closing the door to her present plans and leading her in another direction. After all, if God wants her on the mission field, he will bring in the money. Another candidate, however, might conclude that perhaps he is not working hard enough to raise the money. He might schedule more meetings or work up a better slide presentation. If failure continues, he might simply conclude that other people's decisions not to give have thwarted God's will.

Or consider the Christian college which, after launching a capital-improvement campaign, is finding it difficult to raise money. Some administrators assume that if God wants the new buildings to go up, he will supply the money. Accordingly, if the money does not come in,

---

[1]Bruce Dunn, "The World Will End! The World Will End!" *Moody Monthly,* June 1983, p. 13.

the campaign was not God's will to begin with. Other administrators might emphasize the human element in the situation. If money does not come in, they might conclude that there needs to be a change in development-office personnel. They might also call in consultants to assess the feasibility of raising the needed money and to develop a comprehensive strategy.

Finally, consider a married couple in which the **husband carries a** genetic defect. Should the couple have children? Some might choose to have children believing that each child is a special and direct creation of God. Hence, if God wants them to have a healthy baby, then they will; if he does not, then they will joyfully accept their special child as a gift from God. Other Christian couples might argue that, in view of the high probability that their child will inherit the defect, the responsible thing would be to adopt children or to use their childlessness to offer greater service to the church.

Christians, however, cannot be neatly divided into two camps: those who emphasize divine predestination in their lives and those who emphasize human responsibility. There is also a tendency for Christians to switch back and forth between an emphasis on divine sovereignty and free will as they face different issues. In some situations they talk and, more importantly, act on the assumption that God is in control. They see events in their lives as occurring for a divine purpose; things are the way they ought to be. In other situations the same Christians may talk and act on the assumption that humans are responsible for what occurs. They feel the need to help shape the course of events in the world; things can and should be different.

Examples of this sort of selective application are not hard to come by. Some Christians explain to their children that God "chose to take Uncle John home," yet *at the same time* start an exercise program to insure that they won't die prematurely of a heart attack like Uncle John. Some accept the birth of a radically deformed and mentally deficient baby as a gift of God, yet advocate birth control or adoption to make sure that more children are not born this way. Some thank God for the money he has provided for a Christian institution, yet the next year, when funds fall short, fire the fundraiser and hire a professional firm to plan a new marketing strategy. Some Christian parents thank God for the good jobs he has given their teen-age sons and daughters. Yet they feel obligated to fight racial injustices, believing that many inner-city teen-agers will not get jobs until such injustices are overcome. Some believe that their time of death is appointed by God; yet they have serious reservations about the parents who, on the conviction that God is in control of life and death, refuse to seek medical treatment for their children. Some begin a trip with the prayerful assurance that their safety is in God's hands, yet make sure that the tires are in good shape and the seat belts fastened in order to improve their chances for a safe trip.

These examples make it clear that there are really two distinct but closely related dimensions to the issue before us. On the *theoretical* level, we must decide how to reconcile our belief in divine sovereignty with our belief in human freedom. Just what do "divine sovereignty" and "human freedom" mean? How do they logically relate? On the *practical* level, we must relate our theoretical stance to our lives. Should we live as if God is in total control, or should we live as if humans are free and responsible? Can a justification be given for living out only one of these beliefs? If so, which one? Can switching back and forth between the two be justified? If so, what is to guide us in our selection? These are not idle, academic questions. If we are to avoid arbitrary living, answers must be found.[2]

Outlining the Alternatives
Isolating the various ways Christians respond to the above questions is no easy matter. The alternatives are many and complex. The purpose of this book is to explore four of the perspectives Christians hold on the relationship between divine sovereignty and human freedom. The central question we shall use to introduce these alternatives is this: To what extent does human freedom pose limitations on God's sovereign control over earthly affairs? In response to this question, Christians fall into two camps.

Advocates of Specific Sovereignty. Some Christians believe that human freedom poses no limitations on God's sovereignty. That is, they be-lieve that human freedom in no sense limits God's ability to bring

---

[2]For further discussion of the practical dimensions of this problem, see David Basinger and Randall Basinger, "In the Image of Man Create They God: A Challenge," *Scottish Journal of Theology* 34 (1981): 97-107.

about the specific events he desires. We will call those who hold this belief advocates of specific sovereignty.

Some of these advocates are determinists. Determinists believe that how we act is the result of what has happened in the past. This does not mean, they are quick to add, that we are mindless machines. We consider data, weigh alternatives and make choices. When entering an ice cream parlor, for example, we are not programmed zombies who are unconsciously forced to order a certain flavor. We find out which flavors are available, consider the options and then choose the flavor which is most appealing. But given all the relevant causal factors preceeding the choice, we could not have acted differently. Past events and circumstances bring it about that a certain flavor is in fact ordered. Theological determinists add to this the belief that God has control over all the events and circumstances which preceed any human decision and thus that it is God who ultimately determines what we will do in all cases.

This point of view raises obvious questions. If all our choices are determined by God, how can we be genuinely free? And if we do not choose freely, how can God hold us responsible for our actions? Some theological determinists claim that determinism does rule out freedom of choice and thus are left to explain how God can hold us responsible for our actions. In response, they maintain that we cannot understand—from our finite, human perspective—how God can justly hold us responsible for what he has predestined us to do. It is from the human perspective a paradox. However, since we are clearly taught in Scripture that God is just and that he does hold us responsible, we have no basis for questioning God's justice. We must simply assume that from God's perspective total divine control and human responsibility are compatible. To conclude otherwise is to place human understanding above divine revelation; God would have to bow to a human standard of justice.

Other theological determinists argue that there is a rational way out of this dilemma. They agree that God determines all human choices and activity, but they deny that this is incompatible with human freedom and responsibility. "Determined" individuals can still be considered free and thus responsible for their actions, it is argued, as long as they are doing what they want to do. Consider, for example, a person caught robbing a bank. If she is not robbing the bank because she wants to, but because someone is holding a gun to her child's head, she would not be acting freely. We would not hold her morally responsible because she was forced to act against her will; she was not doing what she wanted to. But let us assume that our robber takes the money because she has decided this is the best way to meet her needs. According to the determinists in question, she could not, given the events of her life, have acted differently. But in this case she was doing what she wanted to do, and thus we can say she acted freely. Accordingly, she can be held morally responsible for her actions. The fact that she was doing what God had decreed she would do does not change this. John Feinberg will be defending a variation of this position.

Other advocates of specific sovereignty deny this deterministic view of human freedom. That is, they deny that what occurs prior to the point at which a decision is made always determines what will be done. They deny, for example, that what has happened in the past necessarily determines what flavor of ice cream I will choose. Given all that has happened before the choice is made, I may well be able to order either vanilla or chocolate. And it is only when people have the ability to act differently in this sense, it is argued, that they are truly free and responsible. Those who accept this view of human freedom are usually called self-determinists or libertarians.

However, if humans are free in *this* sense, how can God be said to be in control? Freedom of this sort would certainly seem to limit God's power. Some self-determinists who believe that God has specific sovereignty respond by an appeal to paradox. They admit that if humans are free and hence responsible for what occurs, it appears that God is not in total control. But we are taught in Scripture that he is. Thus we must assume that, although God does not determine what we will do, he still has total control over all our actions. The relationship between divine sovereignty and human freedom is simply a mystery.

Other self-determinists who maintain that God has specific sovereignty believe that there is a rational answer to this question and that the answer lies in a proper understanding of divine omniscience. God, it is argued, does not determine humans to act in a certain way. But since God is omniscient, he has always foreknown (or timelessly knows) what people will choose to do with their freedom. This allows

God to order his creation in such a way that what humans freely do is always within his specific, preordained plan. In other words, God determines reality in accord with what he foreknows (timelessly sees) will freely be done by humans. Thus humans are free in a self-deterministic sense, yet God is still in total control of the specific events in the world. Norman Geisler, another of our contributors, defends a variation of this view.

Advocates of General Sovereignty. In contrast to these views, some Christians deny that God has specific sovereignty. These Christians believe that human freedom does place limitations on God's control over earthly affairs. These individuals agree with the theological determinist that *if* human actions are determined by God, then God can maintain total control over all events in the world. They believe, though, that our free choices are not determined. In other words, they hold to a self-deterministic (or libertarian) understanding of human freedom. Thus they maintain that to the degree to which God gives us freedom he does not control earthly affairs. In a world like ours, they argue, God has the ability to accomplish general goals. But he cannot assure that all specific events will be in keeping with his will. We shall call those who fall into this camp proponents of general sovereignty.

But how much control does God have in a world with free creatures? On this issue, there is a wide range of options. At one end of the continuum there are those who believe that God cannot bring about any earthly events completely on his own. God attempts to persuade his creatures to act according to his will. While such divine influence does make a difference, God cannot guarantee that any specific event will occur. Process theologians advocate this view of God.

At the other end of the continuum are those who see God retaining a great deal of control over earthly affairs. They argue that God can and frequently does override human freedom or intervene directly in the natural order when he deems it necessary. Thus, they believe that although he has chosen to give humans freedom and thereby cannot control all earthly affairs, he can still achieve his goals by judicious intervention.

Our final two contributors, Clark Pinnock and Bruce Reichenbach, fall within this general-sovereignty continuum. Both affirm that God can intervene in earthly affairs but both deny that he will always ensure that his specific goals will be accomplished. Both see God's decision to give people freedom as imposing significant limitations on his control of earthly affairs. They differ, however, on the degree to which they see human freedom "limiting" divine control. They disagree, for example, on the very important question of whether God knows exactly what will happen in the future. Reichenbach affirms that God has such knowledge. God is never surprised. He always knows what will occur in the world. Pinnock believes that human freedom is incompatible with divine foreknowledge. Thus, God operates in a more "open" universe.

We have not identified the views of our contributors as either Calvinist or Arminian. As a matter of fact, the two proponents of what we have labeled specific sovereignty do consider themselves Calvinists while the two proponents of general sovereignty consider themselves Arminians. But some prominent Reformed thinkers fall into the general sovereignty category while some Arminians appear to affirm specific sovereignty. Moreover, to say that one is a Calvinist or an Arminian is to say *much more* than that one has a certain perspective on the relationship between divine sovereignty and human freedom.

We should also mention why we do not have a contributor representing either of the paradox positions briefly outlined above. It is not because we believe either of these perspectives is less worthy of consideration. But when discussing an issue as complex as the one before us, it is impossible to consider all facets. We have accordingly made the conscious choice to discuss only those positions in which it is claimed that divine sovereignty and human freedom can be shown to be logically compatible.

Finally, let us explain a little about the manner in which the material is presented. As already stated, the problem of divine sovereignty and human freedom arises at two levels: the theoretical and the practical. Accordingly, each of our contributors not only sets forth his theoretical perspective, but also shows the practical implications of this perspective by applying it to two specific case studies (which appear below). One of these case studies is related to a significant global concern; the other is related to a more personal problem. After each contributor's initial essay, the other contributors offer brief critical responses.

We believe that the relationship between divine sovereignty and human freedom is one of the most fundamental and important issues which the thoughtful Christian faces. Yet we feel that there are few issues which cause more confusion. We hope this book will help Christians find some answers or at least provide a context which will enhance this search.

Case Studies

Fred's Case. The family business has grown tremendously since Fred took over. Being a committed Christian who has always believed in God's sovereign control, Fred continually thanks God for this growth and the accompanying material blessings it brings to him and his family.

As a result of some personal reading and a series of meetings at church, Fred has recently become aware of the tremendous poverty in the world and of its complex causes. He has learned how global economies are interrelated. For the first time he realizes that his wealth is not produced in a vacuum; poverty elsewhere in the world may not be wholly unrelated to his wealth. The result of all this is that Fred is finding it harder and harder to know how to pray. Considering the millions who are starving, his prayers of thanksgiving are beginning to sound hollow and selfish. Ought he be thanking God for his own wealth? Is it really God who is responsible for his material blessings? To what extent is his wealth due to the fact that he has been born in a prosperous Western nation? How does God fit into the economic picture? These questions are heavy on Fred's heart and mind.

Mary's Case. Mary is very excited about her new position on the nursing staff of one of the city's finest hospitals. This excitement has helped to ease the bitter disappointment she still feels after having been turned down by several medical schools.

Her pastor has suggested that her failure to make it into medical school might well have been God's way of leading her into something better. While she had earlier recoiled from this suggestion, it is starting to make more sense. Perhaps God does open and close doors in our lives. Perhaps, after all, she should attribute her success in nursing school and the ease with which she obtained her present position to God's direct, sovereign leading. If this is so, then she can rightfully believe that she is in God's will.

Yet Mary has lingering questions and doubts. What if she had stud-
ied a little harder for the entrance exams? What if she had reapplied
as some of her friends had strongly suggested? Or what if she had asked
someone other than Professor Michaels to write a letter of recommen-
dation? (She had been warned about his attitude toward female doctors.) Would things then have turned out differently? Perhaps poor
judgment, others' prejudices and bad timing contributed to her rejection.

But if this is true, where does God fit in? If she could have made
it into medical school, should she now consider herself to be outside
God's will? Has she missed his best for her life? These questions are
causing Mary considerable concern.

I
God Ordains All Things

God Ordains All Things
John S. Feinberg

ARE WE ROBOTS OR ARE WE FREE? WHO'S IN CHARGE IN THE world, we or God? If God foreordains our acts, how can we be morally responsible for them? If God has determined what we will do, must we do it? Such questions have befuddled philosophers, theologians and ordinary people for centuries. For orthodox Christians with unswerving allegiance to Christ and the Scriptures, such questions raise tremendous problems. Few Christians would deny that in some sense God is sovereign over all things, but few as well would deny human free will. How can these two concepts be put together? Is the resolution to this problem beyond human comprehension? Must we simply believe the Bible when it says that God is absolutely sovereign and that we are free, even if we cannot explain how both can be true?

Thankfully, this is not an impossible problem. In fact, there is more than one way to put these concepts together. In this chapter I shall present a moderately Calvinistic model for synthesizing the concepts of divine control and human freedom. This model rests on a view of freedom which is deterministic in nature. Does that sound impossible? Before you conjure up notions of robots, mechanistic universes and fatalism, withhold judgment long enough to let me explain my position.

Statement of Position

Philosophers frequently use the labels *indeterminism* and *determinism* in debates over human freedom.[1] From a theological perspective, Arminians generally incorporate some form of philosophical indeterminism, while Calvinists are usually deterministic. But there is no such thing as *the* definition of indeterminism or *the* definition of determinism. Instead, there are varieties of each.

Indeterminism and Determinism: Basic Notions. In its most basic sense, indeterminism claims that a person's act is free if it is not causally determined.[2] Consequently, the person could always have chosen to do otherwise. While this is a general definition of indeterminism, it can be misleading. For example, it is sometimes taken to mean that no causal conditions whatsoever influence the will. But most indeterminists do not hold this view. Instead, they hold that there are causes that influence the will prior to choosing and that a variety of causal influences may incline the will in one direction or another at the point of decision making. But indeterminists deny that any one cause or set of causes is *sufficient* to determine that a person will choose one thing rather than another. At the point of decision making the various influences produce a stand-off. Some push in one direction and others in another, but none pushes sufficiently to cause the agent to choose one thing over another.[3]

A second misconception about indeterminism is that it assumes that since a free choice is uncaused, it is without a point or reason, and thus random. Choices are made for a reason. The indeterminist's point is that no causal explanation can be given as to why the agent acted according to one particular reason rather than another.[4]

---

[1]This is not to suggest that philosophers have agreed as to which account of freedom is correct. In fact, the debate among philosophers is in many ways a stand-off. Consequently, though there are philosophical arguments for each view, I think the final decision must ultimately be based on scriptural concerns. However, my point at this juncture is simply to note that while Scripture surely teaches human freedom, it does not state what kind of freedom is in view. Thus, one must turn to the philosophical discussion for an explanation of the ways in which human freedom can be understood.

[2]Laurence A. BonJour, "Determinism, Libertarianism, and Agent Causation," *Southern Journal of Philosophy* 14 (1976): 147.

[3]Thomas B. Talbott, "Indeterminism and Chance Occurrences," *Personalist* 60 (1979): 254.

[4]Ibid.

A final misconception about indeterminism is that it means that a causally indeterminate act is not caused by the agent. Indeterminists do not deny that people cause their own actions. Indeterminists merely deny that there is anything which *causes the person* to do the act.[5]

Such, then, is the basic notion of indeterminism. Some philosophers have referred to it as contra-causal freedom.[6] This means that despite the direction in which the causes appear to incline the agent's will, he or she can still choose contrary to those causes, since they do not decisively incline the agent in one direction or another.

Given this understanding of indeterminism, determinism can be seen to differ substantially. The basic notion common to all forms of determinism is the "general philosophical thesis which states that for everything that ever happens there are conditions such that, given them, nothing else could happen."[7] According to this view, for every decision a person makes there are causal conditions playing upon his or her will so as to incline it decisively and sufficiently in one direction rather than another. Consequently, the agent could not have done otherwise, given the prevailing causal influences.[8] Moreover, some determinists say that if one knows the conditions prior to the occurrence of an action or event plus whatever general laws pertain to such states of affairs, one can *predict* what not only may but must happen. For

---

[5]Ibid.

[6]See, for example, Talbott's discussion (in "Indeterminism and Chance Occurrences," p. 257) of J. J. C. Smart's use of the term. Others such as Antony Flew refer to this position as incompatibilism. See Antony Flew, "Divine Omnipotence and Human Freedom," *New Essays in Philosophical Theology*, ed. Antony Flew and Alasdair MacIntyre (New York: Macmillan, 1955).

[7]Richard Taylor, "Determinism," in *The Encyclopedia of Philosophy*, ed. Paul Edwards (New York: Macmillan, 1967), 2:359. Another way to put the point is that for every action or event which is causally determined, there is a state of affairs just prior to its occurrence which, when combined with some causal laws, makes it certain the event or action will occur.

[8]Peter Van Inwagen, "The Incompatibility of Free Will and Determinism," *Philosophical Studies* 27 (1975): 186. Van Inwagen calls those laws the laws of physics. By this term he means a law of nature which is not about the voluntary behavior of rational agents (p. 187). See also BonJour, p. 145; and A. Aaron Snyder, "The Paradox of Determinism," *American Philosophical Quarterly* 9 (October 1972): 353 for a similar definition of causal determinism; also John V. Canfield, "The Compatibility of Free Will and Determinism," *Philosophical Review* 71 (1962): 353-55 for a more formal definition of determinism.

some, then, predictability of actions and events is a logical concomitant of determinism.

Though such notions generally define determinism, important differences emerge among determinists. Consequently, at this point it is necessary to distinguish my form of determinism from forms held by others.

Determinism in the Natural vs. Human Sciences. First, determinism as used in the natural sciences differs from determinism in the human or social sciences. More often than not philosophers and theologians have interpreted determinism in general and Calvinism in particular along the lines of determinism in the physical sciences.[9] Carl Hempel's model for scientific explanation which presupposes determinism is frequently mentioned in contemporary philosophical discussion. His model is known as the deductive-nomological model (or simply the covering law model). Accordingly, if one can set forth a series of sentences which state specific antecedent conditions of an event and then add another set of sentences which represent general laws that cover such instances, one can then deduce and predict the particular event to occur. Likewise, if one begins with the event itself and finds the relevant laws and the antecedent conditions, one can explain why the event occurred.[10]

The importance of this is that while many philosophers maintain that this model is appropriate for the physical sciences, some also have argued for its use in the social and behavioral sciences.[11] My purpose is not to offer a refutation of Hempel or the covering law model (though I think it is inadequate for use in the human sciences).[12] My point is that if one thinks of determinism in terms of the physical sciences, one likely will be led toward a covering law model for the explanation of human action and will probably believe that human

[9]In fact, some of the key items already mentioned such as predictability and general causal laws are germane to determinism in the physical sciences but only dubiously applicable to the social sciences.

[10]Carl G. Hempel and Paul Oppenheim, "Studies in the Logic of Explanation," reprint, from *Philosophy of Science* 15 (April 1948): 135-40.

[11]See for example Carl Hempel, "Rational Action," *Readings in the Theory of Action*, ed. Norman S. Care and Charles Landesman (Bloomington, Ind.: Indiana Univ. Press, 1968).

[12]Compare Alan Donagan, "The Popper-Hempel Theory Reconsidered," *Philosophical Analysis and History*, ed. William H. Dray (New York: Harper & Row, 1966).

behavior is predictable.[13] Such ideas have never been terribly appealing to most of us, and so we have rejected determinism altogether. However, the crucial point is that theological determinism of the kind I am espousing ought *not* to be confused with determinism in the physical sciences. There are antecedent conditions to a person's choice. But more often than not, these conditions are so complex that one could never write all the sentences needed to specify them. Moreover, there do not appear to be general laws covering actions so that one could say "in instances of type A an agent will always choose action x." Such general laws are possible in the physical sciences but not in regard to human actions.

Determinism vs. Fatalism. Second, determinism also is not the same as fatalism. While some hard deterministic positions are equivalent to fatalism, not all are. A position is fatalistic if it claims that there is an inherent necessity in the way things are so that they could not be any other way. Thus, if a person in our world wears glasses, there is no conceivable world God could have created in which that person would not wear glasses. It is inherent in the concept of that person that she or he wear glasses. For a fatalist, the same is true of everything that happens. Fatalists who believe in God claim that even God had no choice but to create the world as he did. The inherent necessity[14] in everything is such that God had to create, and there was only one creative option open to him.

In contrast, I hold that while all things are causally determined, causal determinism does not entail fatalism. I do not hold that what occurs is absolutely necessary in the sense that there is no other way things could happen. Rather, I hold what is known as *consequent necessity*. I believe that once certain choices are made (by God or whomever) certain things follow as a consequence. But before these choices are made, no inherent necessity dictates what must be chosen. For example, it was not absolutely necessary that Adam sin in the sense that there was no other Adam God could have created. Consequently, it was not

---

[13]For discussion of the predictability issue see such articles as Lawrence D. Roberts, "Scriven and MacKay on Unpredictability and Free Choice," *Mind* 84 (1975); Lionel Kenner, "Causality, Determinism and Freedom of the Will," *Philosophy* 39 (1964): 233; and J. Kellenberger, "The Causes of Determinism," *Philosophy* 50 (1975): 445-46.

[14]This is what philosophers refer to as *de re* necessity or absolute necessity.

absolutely necessary that God decide to send Christ as redeemer. However, once having made the choice to create Adam as sinning, it was necessary for God to send Christ as redeemer.

Freedom and Determinism. Third, we must clarify the relation between my form of determinism and human freedom. Indeterminists, of course, assume that causal determinism automatically rules out free human action. But indeterminists usually think no other definition of freedom than their own is possible. That commits the logical error known as begging the question or arguing in a circle. Many determinists also claim that their view rules out freedom. Moreover, since an agent is only considered morally responsible if he or she is free, such determinists claim that no agent is morally responsible.[15] Likewise, many social scientists argue that since we are all products of our heredity and environment, we are not free and thus are not morally responsible for what we do. Such views, however, represent a very hard form of determinism.

Unfortunately, some Calvinists, because of their understanding of God's sovereignty, have denied that humans are free. Yet some of those Calvinists maintain that we are morally responsible for our sin, while God, who decreed our sin, is not morally accountable. When asked how this can be true, they respond that it is a paradox which nonetheless must be true because Scripture demands it.

I do not affirm this paradox. Instead, like many other determinists, I claim that there is room for a genuine sense of free human action, even though such action is causally determined. This kind of freedom cannot be indeterministic, of course. Instead, determinists who hold to free will distinguish two kinds of causes which influence and determine actions. On the one hand, there are constraining causes which force an agent to act against his will. On the other hand, there are nonconstraining causes. These are sufficient to bring about an action, but they do not force a person to act against his will, desires or wishes. According to determinists such as myself, an action is free even if causally determined so long as the causes are nonconstraining. This view is often referred to as *soft determinism* or *compatibilism,* for genuinely free hu-

---

[15]Taylor, "Determinism," p. 368. As Taylor notes, the great American lawyer Clarence Darrow used just such a defense to get many criminals off the hook.

man action is seen as *compatible* with nonconstraining sufficient conditions which incline the will decisively in one way or another.[16]

This notion of freedom seems reasonable if the agent is causally
determined to act as she or he wants to anyway. But what if she is
causally determined to do something she does not desire to do? Moreover, what if God decrees she must act contrary to her wishes? How
can God guarantee that she will freely (in the compatibilist's sense of
freedom) do what he has decreed if she is unwilling? Though this
appears to be an insurmountable difficulty, it is not. A simple illustration will explain how to resolve this matter.

Suppose I decide that a particular student must leave the classroom.
There are at least three ways I can accomplish that. First, if I were
physically strong enough, I could lift the individual and bodily remove
him. In such a case, the student wills nothing; he is a victim, not an
agent. This is an example of the most extreme kind of constraint. The
student's leaving would in no way be considered a free action on his
part.

Second, I could hold a gun to the student's head and tell him to leave
or lose his life. In this case, the student really does not want to leave,
but he does want to live. Unlike the preceding case, he must make a
decision. Being wise, he decides to leave, even though he would prefer
to stay. Here we can talk about the student exercising his will, though
we must admit that he does so under constraint or compulsion. Thus,
even though he acts, the action is not free.[17]

Finally, if I see that the student does not want to leave, I can try to
persuade him that he would be wise to leave. Such persuasion does not
involve threatening, for then I would be constraining him. Instead, I
present reasons why it would be beneficial for him to leave (perhaps
I know that someone outside the room is handing out money to needy
students, for example). Having heard my case, the student reflects on

---

[16]In regard to such freedom, I am not suggesting that no agent ever acts under constraint
(nor does the indeterminist claim that every agent's actions are always contra-causally
free), but only that the basic condition of the will is to act without constraint and thus
freely. If, however, the agent is causally determined by constraining causes on a particular
occasion, I would deny that his act on that occasion was free.

[17]See Antony Flew, "Compatibilism, Free Will and God," *Philosophy* 48 (July 1973): 234
for other examples.

my arguments and his circumstances, and concludes that it would be in his best interests to leave the room. Initially, he had no intention nor desire to leave, but on considering all the relevant factors, his desires changed. He now chooses to leave the room in accord with his changed desires. In this case, the student's action was causally determined, yet it was done (compatibilistically) freely, since the student was not constrained to act against his desires. This is what is meant by soft determinism or compatibilism.[18]

This notion of freedom can easily be applied to the relationship between God's sovereignty and human freedom. God can decree all things and yet we can still act freely in the compatibilist's sense of freedom. God can guarantee that his goals will be accomplished freely even when someone does not want to do the act, because the decree includes not only God's chosen ends but also the means to such ends. Such means include whatever circumstances and factors are necessary to convince an individual (without constraint) that the act God has decreed is the act she or he wants to do. And, given the sufficient conditions, the person will do the act.

Freedom, Determinism, and Doing Otherwise. One final item must be raised in regard to the notion of freedom. Indeterminists argue that no one is free who could not have done otherwise (for indeterminists this means contra-causal freedom). Indeterminists thus claim that determinism removes freedom, because it denies that an agent could have done otherwise.[19] Although this may seem cut and dried, it is not. In particular, soft determinists argue that once we properly understand the meaning of the phrase *could have done otherwise,* there is still room for a genuine sense of freedom.

---

[18]Obviously, this view entails the idea that reasons can serve in some way as causes. I do not wish to debate this here, though it is a debatable point. Suffice it to say that reasons can function to change a person's thinking so that he will then do what is in accord with his reason (this is not to say men always act rationally but only that in the case of a voluntary rather than reflex or involuntary act, they do act for a reason). Such reasons seem to qualify legitimately as part of the sufficient condition which inclines the will. For a somewhat contrary view see A. C. MacIntyre, "Determinism," *Mind* 66 (1957): 37-38; and Charles B. Fethe, "Rationality and Responsibility," *Personalist* 53 (1972).

[19]See, for example, Van Inwagen, "Incompatibility," p. 188; and Susan Wolf, "Asymmetrical Freedom," *The Journal of Philosophy* 77(1980): 154.

The key issue here is the meaning of *can* or *could*. At least seven different things could be meant by the word. First, *can* may be interpreted in the contra-causal sense that no cause or set of causes is sufficient to produce any particular choice on the agent's part. In this sense, the determinist says that someone cannot do otherwise. This is the point of his basic disagreement with the indeterminist. The issue cannot be decided, though, simply by defining freedom contra-causally, as many indeterminists do.

Second, *can* may be interpreted conditionally. According to this interpretation, *the agent could have done otherwise* means she would have done otherwise if she had so chosen.[20] Though some determinists accept this analysis, it really does not substantiate deterministic *freedom*, for it only raises a new objection to determinism, namely, what if the agent could not have *chosen?*[21]

Third, there is the "ability" sense of *can*. Someone may not choose or do a particular action, but has the ability to do so. In other words, nothing is wrong with his faculty of will, and nothing internal or external to him makes it impossible to choose or carry out a particular action. For example, a paraplegic cannot run a mile, even if he chooses to, but a nonparaplegic in good physical shape is able to choose and do the act even if conditions cause him not to.[22]

Fourth, in the "opportunity" sense of *can*, one both has the ability and the opportunity to do something. For example, a young girl may have the ability to jump four feet high, and if she is outside in an open field, she has the opportunity to do so, even if she chooses not to.[23]

Fifth, there is a "rule consistent" sense of *can*. In this sense, there

---

[20] See Wolf, "Asymmetrical Freedom," p. 154 for this analysis.
[21] Ibid.
[22] John Canfield, pp. 356-57. See also Max Hocutt, "Freedom and Capacity," *Review of Metaphysics* 29 (1975) on distinguishing freedom from capacity. It should be noted that there is a sense in which on some occasions even an indeterminist would deny the "ability" sense of *can*. For example, if the agent is asked to actualize a contradiction, even the indeterminist will not argue that even though the agent did not actualize the contradiction, he could have done otherwise. But, this denial of the agent's ability in regard to such a matter hardly counts as a denial of the agent's freedom. Thus, just because someone denies that someone can do other than he has done, does not prove he has denied free will. Consequently, when a determinist says an agent could not do otherwise, one should ask what the determinist means rather than assuming he has denied freedom.
[23] Ibid., pp. 357-58.

is some rule which either permits or prohibits the act a person is able and has opportunity to do. Thus, if rules allow parking in front of a building, a driver can park there, even if something causes him not to.[24]

In the sixth sense of *can* an agent cannot do something because of ill consequences that result from doing it. For example, I cannot (given the negative consequences) drive my car off a cliff, even though I obviously have both the ability and the opportunity, and no rule prohibits me from doing so.[25] Even someone committed to contra-causal freedom cannot do this act in this sense of *can*.

A final sense of *can*, one which seems most appropriate to soft determinism, is the sense in which *can* means "reasonable." In this sense, to say someone can do something means it is reasonable to expect him to do so under the circumstances, and to say someone cannot do something means only that under the circumstances it is unreasonable to expect him to do it.[26] Clearly, if this is the meaning of *the agent could (could not) have done otherwise,* a soft determinist such as myself can agree that the agent could (could not) have done otherwise and still maintain his notion of freedom. Since in this sense of *can* one talks about reasons for doing one thing or another, if those reasons are decisive (and in this case they seem to be), then the action in question is causally determined. But, saying it would be unreasonable for an agent to do otherwise does not mean that his choices are constrained. In fact, it is the very reasonableness of what he chooses which commends the action to him so that he chooses *according to* his desires and thus (on a soft determinist account) freely.

The point is that a soft determinist may interpret *can* in any way except the first and agree with the indeterminist about the agent doing otherwise. If being able to do otherwise is the criterion for being free, then a determinist can legitimately speak of freedom. The determinist has removed freedom from the universe only if one is arbitrarily limited to the first sense of *can*.

---

[24]Ibid., p. 358.
[25]Ibid., pp. 359-60.
[26]This sense is presented by Winston Nesbitt and Stewart Candlish, "On Not Being Able to Do Otherwise," *Mind* 82 (July 1973): 327.

Divine Sovereignty and Determinism

Having clarified my understanding of human freedom, I want to turn now to divine sovereignty. I hold that God is absolutely sovereign, and thus possesses absolute self-determination. This means that God's will covers all things and that the basis for God's sovereign choices is not what God foresees will happen nor anything else external to his will. Rather, God's good pleasure and good purposes determine what he decrees. I also believe that God has chosen at once the whole interconnected sequence of events and actions that have and will occur in our world. Such choices were not absolutely necessary (I reject fatalism), but necessary as a consequence of other choices God made.

This view of God's sovereignty fits nicely with compatibilism. Since God's decree covers all things, it must include both the ends God envisions as well as the means to such ends. God includes whatever means are necessary to accomplish his ends in a way that avoids constraining the agent to do what is decreed. Human actions are thus causally determined but free.

Biblical and Theological Arguments

There are theological and biblical, as well as philosophical, reasons for the position I hold. Given my view of biblical authority, the former must be the decisive considerations. Nonetheless, I shall also present a few philosophical reasons.

Ephesians 1:11. First, I am led to my view by the biblical teaching on God's sovereignty. Though other verses teach divine sovereignty (Ps 115:3; Prov 16:9, 33; Dan 4:34-35), Ephesians 1:11 is perhaps the clearest expression of the notion. This verse is part of the doxology with which Ephesians begins. The basic topic here is our salvation (vv. 4ff.). In verse 11 Paul continues the theme of God's predestining us in Christ for salvation. Paul says that such a marking off of the believer beforehand was done "according to the purpose *[prothesin]* of him who accomplishes all things according to the counsel of his will *[kata tēn boulēn tou thelēmatos autou]*." The clause beginning with *who* is a relative clause modifying *him*. According to this verse, then, believers are predestined to salvation in accord with the purpose of God, and God does all things, including predestining to salvation, according to the counsel of his will. The clause, then, broadens the scope of the verse to speak of God's sovereign control not only over election to salvation, but over all else.

Unless Paul is distinguishing between God's purpose, his counsel and his will, the verse is terribly redundant. Commentators agree that he is making distinctions. The word *prothesin* speaks of the purpose or goal God intends to accomplish. According to this verse, that purpose relates to his predestining to salvation, but surely to everything else as well.[27]

As to the phrase *according to the counsel of his will*, commentators suggest that the distinction between *boulē* ("counsel") and *thelēma* ("will") is that the former involves purpose and deliberation while the latter simply denotes willing. The basic thrust of the phrase is that God chooses after deliberating on the wisest course of action to accomplish his purpose.[28] Thus, in this verse *boulē* refers to a plan resulting from deliberation.[29]

This verse, then, indicates that what occurs is foreordained by God, and nothing external to God such as the foreseen actions or merits of God's creatures determines his choices.[30] God deliberates, chooses and accomplishes all things on the basis of his purposes. How does God accomplish all things? Some are done directly and exclusively by God without use of other agents, but most are accomplished through the agency of others (humans, angels and so on).

Clearly, this verse teaches the absolute sovereignty of God. Just as clearly, with such a notion of sovereignty, I see no room for indeterministic freedom. Given indeterministic freedom, God cannot guarantee that what he decides will be carried out. No matter how much God inclines someone's will toward what he has chosen, such inclination,

---

[27]In the overall context of Ephesians 1 as well as in verse 11 it would be hard to sustain the view that God chooses all things according to deliberation but only has a purpose in regard to his choices to salvation.

[28]B. F. Westcott, *Saint Paul's Epistle to the Ephesians* (reprint ed., Minneapolis: Klock & Klock, 1978), p. 15. See also T. K. Abbott, *A Critical and Exegetical Commentary on the Epistles to the Ephesians and to the Colossians,* International Critical Commentary (Edinburgh: T. & T. Clark, n.d.), p. 20; and John Eadie, *A Commentary on the Greek Text of the Epistle of Paul to the Ephesians* (Grand Rapids, Mich.: Baker, 1979), p. 60.

[29]Eadie, *Commentary on the Greek Text,* p. 60.

[30]Charles Hodge, *Commentary on the Epistle to the Ephesians* (Old Tappan, N.J.: Revell, n.d.), pp. 57-58. See also B. F. Westcott, *Saint Paul's Epistle,* p. 9; and F. F. Bruce, *The Epistle to the Ephesians* (London: Pickering & Inglis, 1974), pp. 29-30.

on an indeterministic account of freedom, can never be sufficient to produce God's decreed action. Given indeterminism, I see no way for God
to be in control of the world as outlined in Ephesians 1:11.[31] On the
other hand, given a soft deterministic account of freedom, not only
does Ephesians 1:11 make sense, but so do such passages as Proverbs
16:9, 33; Acts 2:23; 4:27-28; Philippians 2:12-13; and Hebrews 13:21
(passages concerned with the relationship between divine and human
action).[32]

In response, theological indeterminists may do one of three things.
They may ignore Ephesians 1:11 and similar verses, but that would be
intellectually dishonest. Or, they can try to reinterpret the verse to
mean something other than what it appears to say.[33] Finally, they can
admit that the verse says exactly what I have suggested, but then argue
that though God has absolute sovereignty, he has chosen to relinquish
use of it in order to give us indeterministic free will. Since God has not
given up his sovereignty (but only the exercising of it), and since no
one forced him to give us such freedom, it is still legitimate to claim
that God is absolutely sovereign.

While this final approach certainly maintains God's sovereignty without ignoring Ephesians 1:11, the basic problem is that no passage in
Scripture (certainly not Ephesians 1:11) says that God made such a
decision. If I could find even one verse to that effect, I would be a

---

[31]David Basinger cogently argues this point. I do not agree with his conclusion that we
have to limit God's omnipotence, but I do agree with his analysis of why God cannot
control things given indeterministic free will. See David Basinger, "Human Freedom and
Divine Providence: Some New Thoughts on an Old Problem," *Religious Studies*
15 (1979): 498ff. Others will ask if God cannot control things by determining events
while leaving actions free. For an explanation of the problem with this suggestion see
my "And the Atheist Shall Lie Down with the Calvinist: Atheism, Calvinism, and the
Free Will Defense," *Trinity Journal,* n.s., vol. 1 (Fall 1980).

[32]The point is not that all these verses discuss the same activities, but rather that they
show both God and man operative in the same act in such a way that man genuinely
acts freely while what God wants (and even ordains—Acts 2:23) is most certainly accomplished.

[33]For example, one could claim that the verse refers *only* to predestination to salvation
and nothing else. However, this interpretation will not work for two reasons. First, it
shows a lack of understanding of how relative clauses function grammatically. Second,
on such an interpretation, the indeterminist still must explain how he can make room
for his kind of freedom in regard to salvation, given what the verse says about God's
sovereign control over it.

theological indeterminist (Arminian). Arminians typically offer verses which they think demonstrate that humans have indeterministic free will. While such verses show that we are free, none says we are *indeterministically* free. Indeterminists assume that the verses must mean that we are indeterministically free, because they assume that is the only kind of freedom there could be. But, that begs the question. Actually, no verse tells us whether freedom is indeterministic or deterministic. But, in view of verses such as Ephesians 1:11, I believe we are free in a compatibilistic sense. I see no other scripturally acceptable way to avoid a contradiction between the clearly biblical concepts of God's sovereignty and human freedom.

God's Omniscience. A second argument for my position is the biblical notion of God's omniscience. If indeterminism is correct, I do not see how God can be said to foreknow the future. If God actually knows what will (not just might) occur in the future, the future must be set and some sense of determinism applies.[34] God's knowledge is not the *cause* of the future, but it guarantees that what God knows must occur, regardless of how it is brought about. Of course, if God cannot know the future, questions arise about his omniscience.[35]

Indeterminists typically respond in one of three ways. Some deny that God foreknows the future because the future is unknowable.[36] Such a view is plausible philosophically, but seems inconsistent with biblical theism. The overwhelming testimony of Scripture is that God knows all things, including the future. Consider, for instance, the phenomenon of biblical prophecy.

Another response is to note that God is not in time but eternal. All things are present to him in an eternal, timeless "now." Thus, God

---

[34]The point here rests on a basic definition in epistemology. Knowledge is defined as justified true belief. Consequently, if someone thought he *knew* something but turned out to be wrong, we could not speak of his having knowledge in such a case. Applied to our discussion, the point is that if indeterminism is correct, God cannot guarantee that he knows what I shall do, for I could always do otherwise than he expects me to do. If he really knows, I must do it, but that is inconsistent with contra-causal freedom.

[35]As Stephen T. Davis ("Divine Omniscience and Human Freedom," *Religious Studies* 15 [September 1979]: 303) says, "omniscience includes foreknowledge, which we can say is knowledge of the truth value of propositions about future states of affairs."

[36]Helm discusses this view as he finds it presented in the writings of P. T. Geach. See Paul Helm, "God and Whatever Comes to Pass," *Religious Studies* 14 (1978).

knows all things without knowing the future, since nothing is future to him. Consequently, whatever we do in the future (to us) is still left indeterminate.[37] Though some philosophers from Boethius to our day have accepted such reasoning, I have never been impressed. My point is not that God is in time rather than eternal,[38] but that the view is confused. God is eternal and omniscient, and all things certainly are an eternal "now" to him. However, this does not mean that God does not know what time it is *in human history*. If he knows all things, he knows which things, though present to him, are future *from our perspective*. But, once that is admitted, the same old problem returns. How can God know even as *present* to him something which is *future* to us without that event being determined?[39]

A final way some have tried to answer the problem of freedom and foreknowledge is to appeal to middle knowledge. Middle knowledge is knowledge of counterfactuals; that is, knowledge of what would have happened if something else had occurred.[40] Some claim God knows the future via middle knowledge. Consequently, we can have indeterministic freedom since God does not know what *will* happen, and God can be omniscient in the sense of knowing everything that could happen and knowing what would happen if other things occurred.

---

[37]See for example Richard Purtill, "Foreknowledge and Fatalism," *Religious Studies* 10 (1974). He concludes that if the appeal to God as timeless does not work, we are stuck with the conclusion that God does not infallibly know the future (p. 324).

[38]Davis ("Divine Omniscience," p. 315), for example, denies that God is an eternal being outside of time and argues that God is in time.

[39]It seems that about the only avenue left to the one who would try to resolve the problem with this line of reasoning is to deny the reality of temporal succession. That is, he might simply argue that though it appears to us that there is genuine temporal succession so that one can reasonably talk about a past, present and future, temporal succession is an illusion. Though some might want to argue along these lines, there are few who would find such a view very convincing. At the very least, the implications of denying genuine temporal succession are rather devastating.

[40]Some contemporary philosophers of religion define middle knowledge not only as knowledge of counterfactuals, but also knowledge of what will actually occur in the actual world. If such is what is meant by middle knowledge, however, it will not help the indeterminist's case, for such "middle knowledge" appears to be equivalent to God's foreknowledge of future events, and as has been argued, on an indeterministic account of freedom, it is difficult to say how God could know what actually will occur in the future. Thus, if the indeterminist is to get any mileage out of middle knowledge, he must do so from a conception of it as knowledge of counterfactuals. Consequently, my comments in the text are about that notion of middle knowledge.

Though I agree that God has middle knowledge, I disagree that the indeterminist's problem is resolved. Middle knowledge (as knowledge of counterfactuals) is knowledge of possibilities, not actualities. Since middle knowledge is knowledge of what *might* occur, it is irrelevant to the question of how God can know what *will* happen in the future. Moreover, middle knowledge does not entail that God knows what *could* happen if something else occurred, but rather what *would* happen if something else occurred. However, given indeterminism, how can God *know,* even counterfactually, what *would* follow from anything else unless some form of determinism is correct?[41] Consequently, appeals to middle knowledge do not resolve the indeterminist's dilemma.[42]

Predictive Prophecy. A third biblical argument for my position comes from biblical prophecy. Since prophecy must come to pass, some form of determinism is needed. Scripture foretells the activities of various individuals and groups of individuals.[43] However, if indeterminism is correct, there is no way God can guarantee the fulfillment of any prophecy concerning anyone's future actions; he can do nothing which will causally determine anyone to do what is predicted.[44]

Inspiration. Fourth, given the biblical data in such passages as 2 Peter

---

[41] For an excellent clarification of this issue, see Robert M. Adams, "Middle Knowledge," *The Journal of Philosophy* 70 (1973). See also Basinger's discussion of middle knowledge as it relates to the free will theodicy and God's control of the world ("Human Freedom," pp. 506-8).

[42] Stephen Davis ("Divine Omniscience") offers a fourth resolution (pp. 314ff.). He claims that since incompatibilism is correct, God cannot know the future in the sense of seeing the causal connections that make things causally determined. But, he does know what I, for example, will do (incompatibilistically) freely. He knows it intuitively and immediately. Davis calls this "future vision" and says that it differs from inferential knowledge of the future (based on seeing the causal connections). However, he only explains future vision by saying it is not inferential knowledge. My problem again is how God can even intuitively "see" the future, i.e., what *will* happen, if indeterminism is correct.

[43] Examples include Dan 7; 9:27; 2 Thess 2:3-4; Rev 13:17.

[44] God cannot, for example, guarantee that the man of sin will do what is said of him in 2 Thessalonians 2 or that the 144,000 Jews will in fact respond to accept Christ (Rev 7;14) if incompatibilism is correct. Even if one rejects the futuristic interpretations of these passages which focus on events surrounding the second advent of Christ, one still has the same problem in regard to prophecies about the first advent, for example, which, while already fulfilled, were future to the time of those who wrote them.

1:21 compatibilism seems necessitated by verbal plenary inspiration. The verse says, "men spoke from God as they were carried along by the Holy Spirit" (NIV). The word *pheromenoi* ("carried along") contains the idea of being taken up by the bearer and brought to his goal. The picture is that the biblical writers did not write unless superintended and moved by the Holy Spirit. Such superintendence guaranteed that they wrote his words. If they had continued to write without him, they would have written at their own impulse and initiative, but Peter denies that such occurred (2 Pet 1:20-21). Given the details of this passage, we must accept either a dictation theory, which says God dictated exactly what the writers wrote, or a theory of inspiration consistent with compatibilism, which allows both God and the writer to be active in the process so as to guarantee that what God wanted was written. Given the meaning of indeterministic freedom and all the scriptural evidence against a dictation theory of inspiration, the only way to hold to verbal plenary inspiration as set forth in 2 Peter 1:21 seems to be to hold compatibilism.

Eternal Security. A final biblical argument centers on the eternal security of the believer. If indeterminism is correct, it must always be possible for a believer to reject Christ and lose his salvation. No matter how strong the inclination toward continued faith, believers still must be able to turn away or they would not be free in the indeterministic sense. Traditionally, classical Arminians have seen the point and have argued that a believer could lose his salvation. I, however, find too much biblical evidence which suggests that apostasy is impossible. Passages such as John 6:37-39; 10:28-30; Romans 8:28-30; 1 Corinthians 1:8-9; Philippians 1:6; and 1 Peter 1:5, 9 seem to support the security of the believer. But only a deterministic notion of freedom can guarantee that.

Philosophical Arguments

In addition to the biblical material, let me offer some philosophical reasons for my position beyond those already mentioned. First, I find indeterminism problematic because it claims that although there is no causally sufficient reason for an agent's choices, the agent still chooses. As Jonathan Edwards argued in his *Freedom of the Will*, people act for certain reasons. In particular, they act according to what reason dictates as the greatest good.[45] Thus, if nothing appears to be the greatest good, then the agent does not choose. Herein lies a major problem for indeterminism. On the one hand, indeterminists claim that we do not act without reasons. On the other hand, they deny that any reasons or other causes serve as sufficient conditions for what is chosen. But if nothing is a sufficient condition to incline the will to choose one thing over another, then how do we choose at all? If the causal influences really were at a stand-off, then we would not choose. Moreover, if causal influences are not sufficient to move the will to choose, *then what is?* Some indeterminists claim that a person just chooses. Fine, but on what basis? If the answer is that he or she just chooses, surely this is no explanation at all. If the indeterminist argues that the choice is made in accord with what appears to be the best reason(s), then, in fact, the act is causally determined (reasons have functioned as causes sufficient to produce the act).[46] So, indeterminists are caught in a dilemma. If they reject determinism, then they cannot offer a sufficient reason for an action. If they can offer a sufficient reason for an action, then their view is equivalent to determinism.

A second and related issue concerns moral responsibility for our actions. Generally, indeterminists complain that determinism eliminates moral responsibility. But indeterminism raises problems that are at least as difficult as those raised by determinism. Moral philosophers do not assess moral blame or praise when an act is done either unintentionally or as a reflex. But, if someone does an act intentionally, then surely he does it for a reason or set of reasons which were causally sufficient to move him to act. Therefore, if the only actions worthy of moral praise or blame are intentional acts, and if intentional acts are done in accord with some causally sufficient condition, then we have a strange result; that is, if indeterminism is right, intentional actions

---

[45]Jonathan Edwards, "A Careful and Strict Inquiry into the Prevailing Notions of the Freedom of Will," *The Works of Jonathan Edwards,* vol. 1 (Edinburgh: The Banner of Truth Trust, n.d.).

[46]Some indeterminists appeal to the theory of agent causation, but it runs into the same problem of being unable to specify how agents make their choices without being causally determined. See, for example, BonJour, "Determinism," pp. 148-53 for problems with the agent causation theory.

are ruled out and moral responsibility cannot be assigned.[47]

Objections to Theological Determinism

The most common and crucial objections[48] to a theologically deterministic position focus on moral responsibility: the agent's and God's.

First, how can a person be morally responsible for his or her actions
if they are determined? In order for a person to be morally responsible,
two things must be true. She must be a free agent, and she must be
a moral agent (that is, an agent to whom moral claims apply).[49] According to the indeterminist, determined people can still be moral agents,
but they cannot be considered free. And, if they are not free, they
cannot be held morally responsible for their actions.[50]

Such problems are difficult but not insurmountable. People are morally responsible for their actions because they do them freely. I agree
that no one can be held morally accountable for actions that are not
free. But as has already been argued, compatibilism allows the agent
to act freely. The key is not whether someone's acts are causally determined or not, but rather *how* they are determined.[51] If the acts are
constrained, then they are not free and the agent is not morally responsible for them. But if the act is according to the agent's desires, then
even though the act is causally determined, it is free and the agent is
morally responsible. The indeterminist's objection is fatal only if he can
prove a deterministic notion of freedom to be wrong or impossible.
Since compatibilism is not impossible and has never conclusively been
refuted, the compatabilist can answer this problem about the agent's
moral responsibility for his or her actions.

The second objection focuses on the moral responsibility of God.

---

[47]See, for example, Wolf, "Asymmetrical Freedom," p. 153; and Fethe, "Rationality," p.
196. There is also the problem raised by many that indeterminism amounts to actions
as chance occurrences. But, if actions are random, how can they be free and how can
we be morally responsible for them? For an interesting response to this whole line of
argument see Talbott's "Indeterminism."
[48]Some philosophers raise the Heisenberg indeterminacy principle as an objection
against determinism. For an excellent explanation of the problems with such an argument see Francis A. Gangemi, "Indeterminacy and Human Freedom," *Religious Human-
ism* 10 (1976).
[49]Wolf, "Asymmetrical Freedom," p. 151.
[50]Snyder, "Paradox," p. 353. See also Fethe, "Rationality," p. 196.
[51]Basinger, "Human Freedom," p. 493.

Given the theistic determinist's belief that God decrees all things (even sin), why is God not morally responsible for such sin?[52] It seems unjust that when humans are causally responsible for evil they are also morally responsible, but when God is causally responsible (via his sovereignty) for human sin he is not also morally accountable. Why should God be exempt? And how can a good God decree evil anyway?

This is the more difficult objection. Initially, we must state that God is holy and cannot sin. According to James 1:13-15, God cannot even be tempted to sin. Moreover, God tempts no one to sin nor does he make anyone sin. Sin stems from the creature. God can in no way be implicated in sin. On the other hand, Ephesians 1:11 necessitates that God has decreed all things, even sin. How can that be?

Many theological determinists (Calvinists) have claimed this dilemma is a paradox. They claim that both God's sovereign decree of sin and his absolute holiness must be true because Scripture teaches both. But they cannot explain how they fit together.[53] Though I understand this position, I think it is unnecessary. Some years ago I came to see that the question being asked is really the same question as the problem of evil. This question asks why God should not be held morally responsible for evil since he decreed all things. The problem of evil asks why there should be evil in a world created by an all-powerful, all-loving God. Obviously, if theological determinism is correct, God will not create a world unless he has previously decreed it. But, then, it should be clear that both ways of posing the question amount to this: How can God be seen as holy and just in view of the evil in the world?[54]

In my book *Theologies and Evil* I have offered a detailed response to this question.[55] Here I will simply summarize the main points. The

---

[52]Wolf, "Asymmetrical Freedom," p. 162, makes this point very nicely.

[53]Sometimes appeal is made to Romans 9:18-21 to show that this problem is a paradox and that the believer must not ask for an answer. In verse 19 the intellectual puzzle is raised, and in verses 20-21 Paul responds. But the question posed in verse 19 raises both an intellectual problem and a problem about the attitude of the questioner. In verses 20-21 Paul addresses the problem of attitude, but this in no way suggests that the intellectual question should not be asked or that it is unanswerable. The passage does not really substantiate the paradox position.

[54]I would stress that this is not a Calvinistic point as opposed to an Arminian one. It is simply a point about the logic of the issue.

[55]John Feinberg, *Theologies and Evil* (Washington, D.C.: University Press of America, 1979), chap. 6.

basic strategy of my defense is a strategy used by most theodicists. It begins by noting that even though God is omnipotent, he cannot actualize a contradiction. (For example, he cannot make a square circle.) Theodicists then add that no one, including God, can be held accountable for failing to do what he could not do or for doing what he could not fail to do. This is the basic point that an agent must be free to be morally responsible for his actions. Next, the theodicist postulates two valuable things God could do. However, he notes that God cannot do both together because they contradict one another, and God cannot actualize contradictions. Finally, the theodicist argues that the option God chose is of the greatest value and thus is justified even though it makes it impossible for God to remove evil.

As for my theodicy, I use this strategy and claim that God could either create the sort of beings he created when he created humans (beings who among other things have compatibilistic freedom), or he could maintain a perfect world.[56] God chose to create our world.[57] Therefore, he could not also choose to make a perfect world. Since he could not do both, he cannot be held morally responsible for evil in the world. Creating human beings is of highest value and thus justifies a world in which there is evil.

Practical Applications

Fred's Case. Fred seems to be sensitive both to God and to the needs of others. From my perspective, God decrees all things, including both means and ends. Thus, Fred's wealth, the means to it (including his own hard work), the poverty of others, and the means to that poverty are part of the decree. How, then, should we assess God's control and human effort in this matter of economics?

First, consider Fred's prosperity. He is right to believe that part of

---

[56]The argumentation as to why God cannot remove evil and still leave intact the kind of being he created is offered in chapter 6 of *Theologies and Evil.*

[57]Some will ask whether God should not have chosen the best of all possible worlds. Surely, if there was such a thing, he should have, but on my position on metaphysics (I call it modified rationalism) there is no such thing as a best possible world but only good and evil ones. God's obligation, then, is to create one of those good possible worlds, and so long as one can demonstrate that God has created a good possible world, then he has resolved the problem of evil which arises for his theological system. For more detail see my *Theologies and Evil.*

his wealth comes from being born in a prosperous country. But such matters are also within God's decree. Likewise, the fact that Fred would be prosperous was decreed by God. Since these are not matters of absolute necessity (that is, since this is not a fatalistic universe in which God had to make Fred wealthy), God's choices are expressions of his gracious love to Fred. For all of that, Fred is right in being thankful to God.

On the other hand, God did not "drop the wealth from the sky." Fred had to work hard for it, and he did. But, on my model, Fred's hard work served as the divinely appointed means to his prosperity. Moreover, although Fred's industry should be commended, he must realize that God gave him good health and strength so that he could do his work. Since God owes Fred none of this, and since this is not a fatalistic universe, Fred should thank God for giving him the ability to work hard and then thank God for prospering his efforts. Others work hard but don't always succeed. That Fred has done both is indicative of God's goodness to him. God has been involved in bringing about his wealth, and he is right to thank God.

Second, poverty is also decreed according to my model. Whatever causes such poverty was decreed as the means to the poverty. However, the key point is that those causes did not constrain the individuals in question. For example, if someone brings poverty on himself through laziness or carelessness with money, he was not constrained to do so, and his poverty serves as a punishment. On the other hand, if poverty occurs despite the person's industry, such poverty serves some other purpose of God such as encouraging the individual to rely on God rather than himself. Whatever the cause of such poverty, the poverty is decreed by God and is used by him to accomplish some end, though not necessarily the one we might have envisioned.

Since God has decreed such poverty and the means to it, are the poor morally blameless when their actions or inactivity result in their poverty? On my model they are morally responsible so long as they have done whatever they have done unconstrainedly. Moreover, God is not guilty for their poverty. If human agents do things to bring about their own or others' poverty, God cannot stop them without contradicting his intentions in making them the sort of creatures they are. Likewise, if their poverty occurs as a result of natural evil, then as I have argued elsewhere the question of natural evil reduces either to a problem of moral evil or a religious problem of evil.[58]

Finally, while Fred's wealth may somehow relate to others' poverty, it is doubtful that his wealth is the sufficient condition of their poverty. Fred's having what he has is no proof that he has taken (directly or indirectly) anything from anyone else. Thus, I do not see that Fred should feel guilty for others' poverty (regardless of what one thinks about freedom and sovereignty). But it is proper for him to be concerned about the plight of others. Furthermore, the information he has received about others and his feelings of concern may well be God's leading him to do something to help the needy. In other words, his present thinking (and what has led to it) may be God's appointed means to having him do something to help some of those in need.

Mary's Case. From the standpoint of considering God's will as God's decree, Mary is surely in God's will. In fact, in that sense, everything that happens is according to God's will. On the other hand, one needs to distinguish between God's perfect will and what is often referred to as his permissive will.[59] The former deals with those parts of the decree which are in accordance with God's wishes and his best for us. His permissive will refers to those things which, while in the decree, are contrary to God's desire and what is best for us.[60] Mary's question, then, is not whether what has happened is in the decree, but whether she is in God's perfect will.

On my model, Mary is right in seeing the things which have hap-

---

[58]See my discussion of God and natural evil, chapter 7, in *Theologies and Evil.* There is a basic distinction between a religious problem of evil and a philosophical/theological problem of evil. The former deals with specific instances of evil (not evil in general) which are confronting some individual and affecting his relationship to God. The latter problem is more general. It asks why there should be any evil in a world created by an all-loving, all-powerful God. That question is asked in abstraction from any particular instance of suffering, and it is not about specific evil interrupting someone's relationship to God.

[59]I do not like the term *permissive will,* because it gives the impression that God "steps back" and relinquishes control to man. Nonetheless, it is a fairly typical term even among theologians who are stronger Calvinists than I, and I doubt that we are about to get rid of it.

[60]Though it may appear somewhat strange that God would decree something contrary to his wishes, nevertheless, that is so. Surely sin is contrary to God's wishes, but he decrees it anyway, if Ephesians 1:11 is correct. As to why God would decree something contrary to his wishes, this raises again the problem of evil and the answers to it.

pened (rejection at med school and so on) as the means decreed by God
to getting her new job and convincing her to take it. God has brought
these circumstances into her life to convince her (but not constrain her)
to take the job at this time. If she had not been offered any job, or if
this job had brought untold grief, she might then wonder if she had
taken less than God's best for her. However, the fact that she did well
in nursing school, got the job, and is doing well at it should be confirmation that she has God's best for her, at least at this time.

What about Mary's "what ifs"? Perhaps if she had done some of the
other things mentioned in the case study, she would have been admitted. However, she could just as easily conclude that it was not decreed
that at that time she be admitted, so no matter what she would have
done, she would not have been admitted. Or, she could conclude that
if she had done these things, she would have been admitted, but since
God decreed that she not be admitted, her failure to do these things
was part of God's decreed plan to keep her from med school. Mary may
disagree because she thinks being in med school is God's best for her.
But being in med school could have been wrong for her, even though
now she does not see how.

If my suggestions do not satisfy Mary, there is another option open
to help ease her doubts. Certainly, there are other med schools than
those that rejected her. Let her apply to them. It might not even hurt
to reapply to the first ones. And let her get other recommendations and
study harder for the entrance exam. At the same time, let her ask God
(and really mean it) to close the door again if med school is not his
best for her. She should do everything she possibly can, realizing that
her actions may be the decreed means to getting admitted, and then
she should trust the Lord that the outcome, whatever it is, is his best
for her and the answer to her prayers. If she is rejected again, then she
should be content that God does not want her in med school at this
time (and perhaps never). She should seek to learn what God is trying
to teach her through the whole experience.

What if she is accepted? Would that prove she was out of the Lord's
perfect will up to that time? Not necessarily, for while there is God's
will, there is also God's timing which is part of his perfect will for us.
She may view the rejection as a useless detour, since God wanted her
in med school. But that is because she sees no purpose God could

accomplish in her life by having her rejected from med school and working as a nurse for a while. In fact, though, God may have used this detour to help her appreciate the opportunity more and take it more seriously when she does get into med school. Or, God may have delayed her entry into med school because he has a special position for her which she could not have filled if she had been admitted and graduated from med school sooner. Or maybe God used the detour as a way to get her to ponder the whole matter of knowing and doing God's will. Prior to this incident, she may have basically left God and his desires out of the picture when making decisions about life's work. Now it appears that she recognizes the need to take God and his leading into account.

In sum, whether Mary reapplies or not, she has grounds for thinking she is in God's perfect will. On the other hand, if she still has doubts, I'd encourage her to try again. If she does not get in, she can take it as confirmation that she is where God wants her. If she does get in, she should thank God and seek to discover what he was trying to teach her through the detour. Regardless of what happens, she should thank God for the whole incident. It has clearly made her more sensitive to the need to seek God's leading when facing big decisions.

Norman Geisler's Response

JOHN FEINBERG AND I AGREE ON A LOT OF POINTS. WE BOTH AGREE: (1) that God's providence controls every particular of the universe; (2) that God infallibly knows the whole future; (3) that God has (pre)determined every event; (4) that such a God is not morally culpable for our free choices; (5) that God is eternal, that is, beyond time; (6) that God is immutable in nature and knowledge; (7) that God's election of the saints is eternal and unchanging.

Feinberg and I also agree that even though such a God exists: (1) we are free; (2) we are morally culpable for our own free acts; (3) ought implies can; (4) free choices are incompatible with fatalism; (5) these free choices are made by us.

Furthermore, both of us agree: (1) that sovereignty and free choice are not contradictory; (2) that free choices are sometimes conditioned or limited by external factors; (3) that God never coerces free choices; (4) that God's determining of free acts is not like physical determinism; (5) that free choices which God foreknows are foredetermined; (6) that God cannot both create free creatures and also eliminate all evil at the same time.

In addition to the above agreement, we both hold: (1) that God is absolutely free, having no need to create (p. 29); (2) that God's free choices are "self-determined" (p. 29); (3) that God can "decree something contrary to his wishes" (desires) (p. 41, note 60).

But in spite of this large area of agreement, there appear to be some important areas of difference between our views. My basic problem with Feinberg's view is that, logically, it amounts to a denial of human free choice and, thus, would make God responsible for evil.

The first problem I see with the position is that Feinberg holds that God can decide (choose) contrary to his desires but we cannot. If this is so, then God is free and we are not. Feinberg rejects the view that an agent can "act against his will, desires or wishes" (p. 24). For he claims that even if "initially, he had no intention nor desire to leave . . . his desires changed" [by God's causality]. Thus, Feinberg insists that the agent "was not constrained to act against his desires" (p. 26). For him this is so in spite of the fact that he admits that the person "really does not want" to do it in the first place. Thus for Feinberg, an act is according to the agent's desires, even though the act is causally determined by God (p. 35). But if God causally determined it against what the agent "really" desires, then how can we blame the agent for doing it?

Feinberg identifies his view with Jonathan Edward's position, adding that unless God gives the change of desire (will), there is no "sufficient condition to incline the will to choose one thing over another" (p. 33). These conditions function as "causes sufficient to produce the act" (p. 33). Feinberg believes that unless there is such a causally sufficient condition there will be nothing to cause the action. But if this reasoning is right, then God would not be able to act freely either. For there is no causally sufficient condition beyond his will for his choices. But Feinberg admits God can act freely. Therefore, Feinberg's view is inconsistent. Granting that *freedom* means the same thing in each case, he must either admit that God's acts are not free or else that our free actions, like God's, are self-determined. Of course, Feinberg could easily correct this problem by applying his concept of God's self-determining freedom to us who are made in God's image.

Second, Feinberg believes that all acts must be causally determined by God, yet he holds that God does not coerce us. But is this possible? The difficulty is concealed behind some euphemisms such as "incline decisively" (p. 25), "changed desire" (p. 26) and "guarantee" the outcome (p. 26). But how can God decisively guarantee the result without forcing or coercing the individual? What if individuals reject the non-coercive impulse God gives? What if they decide not to allow this new desire to rule them? Feinberg responds elsewhere by claiming that God "did not create men's actions themselves."[1] That is, God gives the power of choice to humans but leaves the performing of the actions up to them. But if this were so, then we would be free to reject the persuasion or desires which God offers us. If Feinberg admits that we can decide contrary to these God-given desires, however, then his view collapses.

If Feinberg answers that the God-given desire is coercive, then he has fallen into the hard determinist view which he rejects. Once a free choice is made not to accept the wooing, moving or reasoning which God offers, then there is no way on Feinberg's grounds for God to "guarantee" the outcome without forcing the free act. But Feinberg admits that forced freedom is a contradiction. Therefore, to avoid this contradiction Feinberg would have to accept a view in which predestination works by persuasion without coercion, in accordance with human free choices. This is the view which I embrace.

Third, most of Feinberg's either/or arguments between determinism and indeterminism are answered by his own acknowledgment of a third category of freedom (self-determined) which he applies to God. But if there are three categories, then his dilemmas are false ones and his conclusions do not follow. Feinberg provided no refutation of the view that human free choices are self-determined. Indeed, any argument against self-determinism would prove too much. It would prove that Feinberg's concept of God's self-determinism was wrong too.

Of course Feinberg could always deny that there is any similarity between God's freedom and human freedom. But if the term *freedom* is used equivocally of God and us, then why call us free? Why not simply admit, as hyper-Calvinists do, that we are not really free? In fact, in spite of his description of himself as a "moderate Calvinist," Feinberg's view really reduces to a strong Calvinistic determinism in which we are not actually free at all. According to this view, we cannot actually choose contrary to the desires which God gives us. Indeed, believers cannot do other than what they do. They can do only what they desire,

---

[1]Feinberg, *Theologies and Evil*, p. 123.

and only God gives those desires.

Finally, Feinberg seems to confuse efficient causality with final causality. He assumes (wrongly) that the cause of free choice is a "reason." But the agent (the self) is the efficient cause of a free act and not the reason or purpose (final cause). For example, who created the world (efficient cause) is a different question from why (final cause) he created it. The purpose (reason) for acting no more causes the act than the desire to have a chair produces a chair. It takes a carpenter (efficient cause) to produce a chair, not simply the desire to sit down. Furthermore, both Scripture (Rom 7) and experience show that one is free to reject even the best of desires or reasons.

Another way to state the problem is that Feinberg confuses condition and cause (sufficient condition). He shows rightly that God conditions human choices. But to go beyond this and declare that God is "causally determinative" of the choice is to say that it is no longer our choice. What one needs to say is that God is determining moral actions by his knowledge of what, by unfettered free choice, we are causing to happen. In this case our actions are self-caused (that is, caused by us), even though God determinately knew (and knowingly determined) we would so choose. But Feinberg rejects this option and thus confuses the precondition of a free act with its cause, a free agent. But conditions are no more the cause than dry leaves are the cause of a forest fire. They are merely a precondition. Likewise, God-given desires, reasoning and persuasion can be conditions of a free choice. But they are not the cause. That is, they are not the sufficient causal condition of our action. If they are, then the human agent is not the efficient cause of the action, but only the instrumental cause through which God's action is exercised. But in this case then the moral blame falls on God. In this case Feinberg's view is not really different from the hyper-Calvinist view he wants to avoid.

Bruce Reichenbach's Response

THE SPACE ALLOTED TO OUR REPLIES CANNOT DO JUSTICE TO JOHN FEIN-berg's clearly argued presentation. The reader will have to refer to my own and Clark Pinnock's chapters to get a full sense of the arguments in support of the contrasting view. However, let me say a few words about both his position and the arguments he gives in support of it.

His Position
Feinberg argues, on the one hand, that determinism is true. That is, for everything that happens or exists—for all events (p. 22) and things (p. 38)—there are sufficient causal conditions. On the other hand, he wants to maintain that, though our decisions are determined in that there are causal conditions which "incline [the will] decisively and sufficiently in one direction rather than another," (p. 21) there are times when we are free. We are free when we are not constrained by these causes to act contrary to our desires. What this means is that though we are caused to act as we do, we are free with respect to a given act if and only if that act is what we would have done or chosen to do, even if the sufficient causes had not been present.

Further, he contends that God decrees (wills) everything that happens. His decrees follow the purposes and desires which God alone determines. When the action we perform is both what God has decreed and what we desire, we act freely. But what if our desire does not accord with God's decree? Feinberg contends that God, having decreed everything, knows what factors and circumstances will noncoercively persuade us to choose what God decrees.

Several serious problems arise with this position. First, how can persuasion *guarantee* that the person will want to act in accord with God's decree? The guarantee cannot be effected in any causally coercive manner, for that would remove our freedom. It must operate then in a nonconstraining manner. Feinberg indicates that it operates through reasons which, among other things, appeal to our self-interest.

But are good reasons, even reasons appealing to self-interest, always effective in altering our desires? Feinberg must say yes to this, or else God has none but coercive tools to change our desires. But reflect on the many instances in which people simply cannot be persuaded to change their minds, either by reason or appeal to emotions or self-interest. Feinberg must assert that all persons ultimately and noncoercively can be persuaded to God's perspective (as found in his decrees), and that as omniscient, God would know what would be persuasive in those cases where the person would dissent.[1] But if everyone can be persuaded to God's perspective on any point, why does not God decree that everyone not only always do good but acknowledge him as God?

In fact, many people do evil and not all will be saved. What of those who do evil? It follows from Feinberg's position that it is possible that God has to persuade someone to do evil. This sounds absurd, but consider what follows from his view of authority. According to Feinberg, God has at one time decreed all that comes about. This means that God has decreed the evil as well as the good. Further, this is done prior to and independent of any human action. Now suppose that someone desires to do good rather than the evil which God has decreed he do, or to accept God rather than reject him as God has decreed. Since all must occur as God has decreed, God is put in the indelicate situation of persuading the individual that it is rational and in his best interests to do evil rather than good or to reject God rather than accept him.

---

[1]This position presupposes that God has knowledge of what we would do if something other than what takes place occurred; that is, that God has knowledge of counterfactual conditionals of free will. In my chapter in this book I have argued to the contrary that neither God nor mankind can have such knowledge. See my discussion there.

God's sovereignty has been protected, but at the cost of his wisdom and goodness.

Secondly—and this strikes at the heart of every compatibilist position—if every event and thing is caused, then my very choices, beliefs and desires are caused. But if my choosing and desiring are caused by causes which ultimately can be traced back prior to the existence of the individual human person, I cannot will, choose or desire other than I am caused to do. But then the freedom asserted by Feinberg is an illusion, for there is no sense to his analysis of freedom given in terms of what the person would have done or chosen to do even if the causes had not been present, for there are *no* events where there are no sufficient causes present.

Further, on Feinberg's theistic compatibilism, my desiring and choosing must be decreed by God, since my having a desire and choosing are events. Thus there is no instance in which I can desire anything other than that decreed by God. Should I desire other than that decreed by God, that very desire is itself decreed by God. Again freedom becomes an empty notion, for there can be no desire independent of God's decree.

Finally, there is no need for divine persuasion, for all attitudes and desires cannot but be in accord with the divine decrees if everything is as decreed by God.

The picture Feinberg paints in the case studies is misleading. He suggests that Mary can ask God to close the door to medical school, submit to God, and be content with what she has, as if her asking, submitting and other mental acts, like desiring to be in God's will, somehow were dependent on her. But if everything is determined by causally antecedent conditions, what she wants and desires depends on those conditions, not her. And if everything is decreed by God, there can be nothing contrary to that decree. As such, her freedom to ask, submit, be content, and desire to be in God's will is an illusion. If God decreed she be content, she cannot but be content; and if God decreed she submit, she cannot but choose to submit. There is no contrary state from which she is to be persuaded, or if there is, both that contrary state and the persuasion are decreed by God. But then there is no independent state of Mary's (like desiring, submitting and so on) from which one can measure God's decrees to see whether she was free.

Thus, her freedom is an illusion.[2]

His Arguments

Feinberg develops five theological and two philosophical arguments to support his compatibilist position. The first theological argument is that this particular view of divine sovereignty is found in Scripture, particularly in Ephesians 1:11. Admittedly, if this were the only passage we had on the subject of divine sovereignty, some sort of strong predestinarian view would be called for. But there are more passages than this one. Readers should refer to my chapter in this volume.

Two other points might be made, however. First, there are other passages in the New Testament which ground election on divine foreknowledge.[3] Second, when Ephesians 1:11 states that God "works out everything in conformity with the purpose of his will," there is a critical ambiguity which Feinberg overlooks. Does the passage teach that God does or works out *everything* in conformity with his purposes, or does it teach that *everything* God does he does in conformity with his purposes? The grammar of the sentence does not force us to adopt one interpretation over the other. For example, one can say, "John does everything very slowly." From this we would not infer that John does

---

[2]Professor Feinberg's suggestion that she try again to get into medical school in order to get "confirmation that she is where God wants her to be" is most puzzling. Why should she only try one more time? Should she not try a third time to confirm the first two? God might have decreed that she would make it on the third application. And if she fails the third time, should she not try a fourth time to confirm the first three . . . and so on? Why should she be content that "God does not want her in med school at this time" rather than that she try again? In short, contrary to Feinberg's hints, her failure to be accepted tells her nothing about her relation to God's will and God's best or about what she should do next. It only tells her that God has decreed that *this* time she not be accepted.

Further, one must reject his distinction between God's perfect and permissive wills. On the one hand, we are told that God's decrees stem from his purpose and pleasure (p. 30); on the other hand, we are told that God decrees things which are contrary to his desire and to the best for us. One can see no reason why God would decree anything contrary to what he desires and what is best for us.

[3]Rom 8:29; Acts 2:23. Acts 2:23 is ambiguous about the relation between God's set purpose and his foreknowledge. Of course, foreknowledge in these passages is not simply intellectual knowledge, for as has been often pointed out, knowledge in Scripture is experiential. Nonetheless, this does not invalidate the relation established in these passages.

everything, only that everything he does he does slowly. Similarly, one cannot infer from this verse that God does or works out everything; it is just as reasonable to interpret this passage as asserting that all of God's acts proceed from his counsel.

Feinberg's second argument is that, given the indeterminist view of human freedom, God cannot foreknow the future. The reason for this is that the future, on the indeterminist view, is at any given time indeterminate. A person could either perform a particular action or refrain from performing it. Only if the future is set can God know it.

But this would be true only if we deny that God's knowledge is truly *fore*knowledge. To have foreknowledge is to know what will occur prior in time to its occurrence. If knowledge is defined as Feinberg suggests, namely, justified true belief, then you and I have foreknowledge. For example, I knew yesterday that I would arise this morning between 7 and 8 A.M. Yesterday I had this belief, and this belief was true (I did in fact arise at 7:15 A.M. this morning), and the belief was justified—based on a good inductive inference from my past behavior on workday mornings. Yet I was not caused to arise at this time (though I had reason to do so); I could have arisen at a later time or not arisen at all. I could have done other than I did this morning (in the indeterminist sense of *could have done other than I did*).

God's foreknowledge, of course, differs from mine, not in its being foreknowledge, but in the ground of his knowledge. My foreknowledge is based on inferences from past experience, whereas his is grounded in the event itself. As such, what God knows is what human persons actually do. But this knowledge does not determine the actions we perform. It is based on those very actions. Thus the future is, as Feinberg suggests, "set," but in a very trivial way: we will do what God knows we will do, which is to say, we will do what we will do. But that still leaves us free (in the indeterminist sense) to do or not to do.

Feinberg's third argument concerns prophecy. How, he asks, can God guarantee the fulfillment of prophecy if the future is open to us to do or refrain from doing? The answer follows from God's foreknowledge. What needs to be guaranteed, contrary to Feinberg, is not the event prophesied but the prophecy. And the prophecy is guaranteed because of God's foreknowledge of the event itself.

Fourthly, he argues that, based on 2 Peter 1:21, plenary verbal inspiration requires a compatibilist view of human freedom. For one thing, it might be doubted whether 2 Peter 1:21 teaches plenary verbal inspiration. What it does say is that prophecy (not all Scripture) orig- inates from God, not man. It does not say that the expression of that prophecy in human language was such that God controlled every word. More generally, however, one might argue that Scripture does not teach the particular view of inspiration which Feinberg advocates. It does teach inspiration (2 Tim 3:16), but the doctrine of inspiration can be understood in terms of God's revelation to writers whom he moved to write. As such, in many cases God's revealing activity and controlling of the outcome is in terms of necessary and not sufficient conditions. It need not be thought to extend to the words used or style employed, but rather to the truths presented.

Finally, Feinberg argues that the doctrine of eternal security entails that the indeterminist view is false. If the believer is able to do what he wills, he could apostasize following his reception of God's grace. But is the doctrine of eternal security either biblical or true? There is not space to argue the view, but many passages in Scripture teach that apostasy is possible and must be guarded against (Heb 6:4-6; 10:26- 29; Lk 8:6-7, 13; Jn 15; Rom 11:22; Rev 3; Acts 5:1-11).[4]

As to his philosophical arguments, both rest on the thesis that the indeterminist can provide no *causally* sufficient reason for our choices or actions. Consequently there is neither an explanation for our actions nor any way to ascribe moral responsibility for our acts. But why must all explanations of human action be causal? To assert that they must be causal is to beg the question.

Contrary to Feinberg, it is legitimate to say that a person can have a sufficient reason for doing a certain act without that sufficient reason functioning causally. In my going to the store to buy a gallon of milk, the purchase of the gallon of milk did not cause my going, though it is the reason for my going.

In sum, the compatibilist attempt to reconcile determinism and hu- man freedom is unsuccessful. On its view freedom turns out to be an illusion. Similarly, the attempt to reconcile a divine determinism of all

---

[4]For an extended, careful treatment of the topic, see Robert Shank, *Life in the Son* (Springfield, Mo.: Westcott, 1960).

events with human freedom is doomed to failure. We must abandon the model which sees God as the cosmic novelist; God seeks not to determine our existence, but to love us into a free acceptance of his gracious salvation and a meaningful, developing and deepening relationship.

Clark Pinnock's Response

FROM MY READING OF BOOKS, I HAVE ALWAYS KNOWN THAT DIE-HARD Calvinists existed. But I had not expected to run into one like Feinberg in the late twentieth century. What an interesting essay this is—so admirable in logical coherence but so dismal in what it actually proposes. Here we have a medicine much worse than the ailment. Better to leave sovereignty and freedom unresolved than to explain their relationship in this manner.

Like my own essay, Feinberg sees some things very clearly. He recognizes that complete divine omniscience of all future states would rule out genuine freedom. He senses that timelessness will not work as a solution. But then tragically he clings to the deterministic model of God's sovereignty and sweeps all contingency and novelty from the universe. Rather than reconsider the frozenness of his theism, he chooses (causally determined, I presume!) to indict God for all the evil he deliberately decreed and to deny us the freedom which makes our life on earth distinctive and precious. There is one thing at least for which the reader can be thankful. The author's presentation is so honest and straightforward that he virtually refutes his own position by failing to offer convincing solutions to the gross problems he admits burden it.

Feinberg's big mistake lies in following Augustine and thus thinking that God decrees and controls everything that happens in history down to the last detail. He even shrinks from saying that God only "permits" some atrocity like the Holocaust, as some less stout Calvinists inconsistently do, because this would suggest it originated outside God's sovereign will. Far be it from the Calvinists to deny God the glory of causing everything! It should be clear to the reader why the number of strict Calvinists is relatively small. It involves one in agonizing difficulties of the first order. It makes God some kind of terrorist who goes around handing out torture and disaster and even willing people to do things the Bible says God hates. Some time ago a madman murdered twenty people in a McDonald's near San Diego. According to Feinberg, although God does not like this sort of thing, he decreed it anyway. Wouldn't it be simpler just to say God does like it and retreat into dark mystery? Feinberg says that space does not permit him to give a good answer and refers us to his book. He will have to forgive me for thinking this a cop-out and that however long his book there is no way to clear God's reputation in such a case. One need not wonder why people become atheists when faced with such a theology. A God like that has a great deal for which to answer.

In my view the Bible does not teach this. Of course God energetically pursues his will for the world in all areas, as Feinberg's proof text says (Eph 1:11). But that does not mean God's will is actually done in every case. Quite the contrary. Jesus made it plain that the Pharisees "rejected the purpose of God for themselves" (Lk 7:30). They were not in a position to thwart God's will for the whole world, but they were able to reject it effectively in their own case. God is not willing that any should perish—yet some do. God does not want husbands to beat their wives—yet some wives are beaten. God desires all to be saved, but all are not saved. Jesus longed to gather the Jews as a mother hen gathers her chicks, but they were not willing. God did not want them to resist the Spirit, but they did resist him. It is hard for me to imagine why Feinberg would accept a view of divine sovereignty which so contradicts the general tenor of Scripture. According to the Bible, men and women can and do reject God's will and plan. God in his sovereignty has given to them this dread power. Contrary to Calvin and Augustine, God's will is *not* always done.

The price Feinberg is willing to pay for his mistaken view of divine sovereignty is even higher than ruining God's reputation. He is compelled to accept a view of human freedom which few readers, I would guess, will be able to accept. In every moment of decision, he says, there is a set of circumstances which render it certain which way the choice will go. Individuals are determined to follow the strongest desire within them. They are causally determined and yet free! They may feel that genuine alternatives lie before them and that there is some indefiniteness in the air, but it is not so. What was divinely decreed from all eternity is what will infallibly happen.

I suspect that many readers will agree with me that we are being cheated here. What Feinberg is pleased to call *freedom* does not deserve the name. Let me use an example to make it clear. Joseph robs a bank. He did not have to do it. Nobody made him do it. But he felt like it. His background and desires were such that robbing the bank at that moment was inevitable. He couldn't help himself. Joseph was a victim of causal factors over which he had no control. A doctor might try to reprogram him, but no judge has a right to condemn him for doing what he could not help. Any sense of moral responsibility just flew out the window with Feinberg's definition of freedom. The Bible presents a very different world from this. In it people make choices which determine the future in ways not determined already by the past. They make weighty decisions which involve them in the realm of moral responsibility. All this is clear both in the Bible and in ordinary life. But Feinberg is willing to give it all up just to hold onto a view of divine sovereignty which itself is mistaken. It is a tribute I suppose to his tenaciousness in clinging to the old Augustinian theology.

The practical implications of Feinberg's view for Fred and Mary are predictable. Neither of them, nor indeed anyone anywhere, needs to worry about being in the will of God. How, given this view of deterministic sovereignty, could anyone fail to be in God's will? That is the whole point of Feinberg's world view. God's will is always done. The rich man in his castle; the poor man at his gate—God decreed history to fall out that way. God willed whatever happens. It would be irrational to worry about anything in the Calvinist's universe. Just submit to the deterministic will of God! If God wants to save you, he will certainly do so, and without your lifting a finger to help him. If he wants you poor, you might as well get used to it, because there is no changing it. Fred need not worry about the morality of his wealth since the reality of moral responsibility has flown out the window. Mary need have no lingering doubts because everything that happens was meant to be.

From my point of view, of course, Fred and Mary are correct to sense that God's will is a dynamic affair and not set in stone. They are right to think things could have gone one way or the other. It is good that they are pondering how God's ideal will for them can be more perfectly realized than at present. Calvinistic thinking on such matters is remote from the actual experience of real people, even when they are Calvinists, and this is yet another reason for suspecting Calvinism is wrong.

II
God Knows All Things

God Knows All Things

Norman Geisler

THE FAMOUS FRENCH EXISTENTIALIST JEAN PAUL SARTRE ARGUED: If God exists then the future is determined and I am not free; I am free; therefore, God does not exist.[1] In contrast, the great Puritan theologian Jonathan Edwards argued: If every event has a cause, then so do free human choices; God is the First Cause of everything; therefore, God must be the cause of our free choices.[2] Sartre used freedom to eliminate God, and Edwards seemed to use God to eliminate freedom. Since the biblical Christian grants both God's sovereignty and human responsibility for free choice, there remains the problem as to how to reconcile them.

The Biblical Data

Divine Sovereignty. The Bible clearly teaches that God is in control over the entire universe, including human events. God's general sovereignty is revealed in numerous passages. For example, Job declared of God: "I know that you can do all things; no plan of yours can be thwarted" (Job 42:2, NIV used throughout this essay). The psalmist acknowl-

---

[1]Jean Paul Sartre, *Being and Nothingness,* trans. Hazel E. Barnes (New York: Washington Square Press, 1966), pt. 4, chap. 1.

[2]Jonathan Edwards, "Freedom of the Will," in *Jonathan Edwards,* ed. Clarence H. Faust and Thomas H. Johnson (New York: Hill and Wang, 1962), p. 305.

edged that "the LORD does whatever pleases him, in the heavens and on the earth, in the seas and all their depths" (Ps 135:6). Solomon said, "The king's heart is in the hand of the LORD; he directs it like a watercourse wherever he pleases" (Prov 21:1).

John's exultation in the Apocalypse acknowledged of God: "You are worthy, our Lord and God, to receive glory and honor and power, for you created all things, and by your will they were created and have their being" (Rev 4:11). As Paul put it in Colossians, "He is before all things, and in him all things hold together" (1:17). God not only controls what comes to exist or continues to exist, but he directs the very course of things that do exist. According to Scripture, God "works out everything in conformity with the purpose of his will" (Eph 1:11). God said to Pharaoh, "I have raised you up for this very purpose, that I might show you my power and that my name might be proclaimed in all the earth" (Ex 9:16). This same divine control is exercised over all creation, including all angels whether good or evil (Job 2:1; Phil 2:10).

God's sovereignty is not only exercised in general over his creation, but it is manifested in particular matters of human redemption and salvation. Even Christ, the sole means of salvation (Acts 4:12; 1 Tim 2:5), "was handed over . . . by God's set purpose and foreknowledge" (Acts 2:23). Ephesians says that God "chose us in him [Christ] before the creation of the world" (1:4). Luke declares that "all who were appointed for eternal life believed" (Acts 13:48). And in perhaps the strongest of all passages on divine sovereignty the apostle Paul boldly declares that salvation "does not, therefore, depend on man's desire or effort, but on God's mercy." Therefore, "God has mercy on whom he wants to have mercy, and he hardens whom he wants to harden" (Rom 9:16, 18).

Human Responsibility. The Bible also declares that individual persons are responsible for their moral choices and even their eternal destinies. Adam and Eve were commanded not to eat the forbidden fruit (Gen 2:16-17). When they disobeyed, God demanded: "What is this *you* have done?" (Gen 3:13). Adam admitted, "*I* ate it" (v. 12). God concurred, saying, "Because *you* listened to your wife and ate . . ." (v. 17).

Throughout the Bible God calls on people to exercise a choice. Joshua charged Israel, "*Choose* for yourselves this day whom you will serve" (Josh 24:15). Elijah prodded Israel asking, "How long will *you*

waver between two opinions?" (1 Kings 18:21). Indeed, Jesus held his
people responsible, crying, "O Jerusalem, Jerusalem . . . how often I
have longed to gather your children together . . . but *you were not
willing*" (Mt 23:37).

In fact, even our state of ignorance and depravity is said to be willful.
Peter said, "They *deliberately* [willfully] forget [what God said]" (2 Pet
3:5). Romans declares, "You are slaves to the one whom *you obey*—
whether you are slaves to sin, . . . or to . . . righteousness" (Rom 6:16).
Even the pagan world which knew the truth about God by general
revelation was held to be "without excuse" before God because they
"suppressed" the truth (Rom 1:18-20). And spiritual blindness came to
those who chose to be "unbelievers" (2 Cor 4:3-4). According to Paul
both "darkness" and "ignorance" of the truth are because of the hard-
ness of their heart (Eph 4:18). Even the strong passages on God's
"hardening" Pharaoh's heart follow only after Pharaoh first repeatedly
hardened his own heart (Ex 7:13-14, 22; 8:15, 19, 32). Indeed, the last
verse says "This time also *Pharaoh hardened his heart.*" And when Paul
spoke in Romans 9 of "objects of his wrath—prepared for destruction," he implied that this was a result of their free choice of stubborn
rejection which God "bore with great patience" (v. 22). For as Peter
said, "He is patient with you, not wanting anyone to perish, but everyone to come to repentance" (2 Pet 3:9).[3]

Both Sovereignty and Responsibility. The Scriptures emphatically declare that God is in complete control of all that happens, including the
salvation and condemnation of all people. Nevertheless, the same Scriptures stress that the responsibility for moral action rests squarely with
free moral agents and not with God. In fact, sometimes the tension of
these two truths is expressed in the same passage. Consider the mys-
terious relation of God's sovereign will and culpable, free human
choice in the following passage: "This man [Jesus] was handed over to
you by God's set purpose and foreknowledge; and *you . . . put him to
death* by nailing him to the cross" (Acts 2:23). Both sides of the divine
sovereignty and human freedom picture are manifest in Jesus' statement, "All that the Father gives me will come to me, and *whoever comes*

---

[3]For an insightful treatment of the biblical passages on predestination, see Roger T.
Forster and V. Paul Marston, *God's Strategy in Human History* (Wheaton, Ill.: Tyndale,
1973).

to me I will never drive away" (Jn 6:37).

There is another interesting passage in Acts which states that "all who were appointed [by God] for eternal life believed" (Acts 13:48). Yet within a few verses of this text Luke says, *"They spoke so effectively that a great number of Jews and Gentiles believed"* (Acts 14:1). So the Bible teaches both divine sovereignty *and* human responsibility, often in the same passage.

Theological Views

Evangelical Christians have attempted to explain the relationship between God's sovereign predetermination (predestination) and human free choice in three basic ways. These three views are represented by Arminians, strong Calvinists and moderate Calvinists.

God's predetermination is based on his foreknowledge. Some evangelicals believe that God knows in advance (by his omniscience) just what choices everyone will make, for example, whether to accept or to reject salvation. Hence, on the basis of their foreknown free choice to accept Christ, God chooses (elects) to save them. Thus humans are totally free to accept or reject God, being under no coercion from him. On the other hand, since God is all-knowing, he is in sovereign control of the whole universe because he knew exactly what everyone would choose to do, even before he created the world. In short, humans are entirely free and yet God is in complete control of the universe. But the "control" is not based on coercion of the events but on *knowledge* of what the free agents will do.

This view faces several problems. First, the biblical data seem to say more than God simply *knew* what was going to happen. Scripture seems to say that God actually *determined* what was going to happen and that he even assures its accomplishment by effectively working to bring it about. Paul was "confident of this, that he who began a good work . . . will carry it on to completion until the day of Christ Jesus" (Phil 1:6). He added, "It is God who works in you to will and to act according to his good purpose" (Phil 2:13).

Second, if God's choice to save was based on those who chose him, then it would not be based on divine grace but would be based on human effort. This flies in the face of the whole biblical teaching on grace (compare Eph 2:8-9; Tit 3:5-7). And it is contrary to the clear teaching of several passages of Scripture that salvation does not spring from the human will. John said believers are "children born not of natural descent, *nor of human decision* or a husband's will, but born of God" (Jn 1:13). Paul adds, salvation does not "depend on man's desire [will] or effort, but on God's mercy" (Rom 9:16).

Finally, the whole idea of there being a chronological or even logical sequence in God's thoughts is highly problematic for evangelical theology. It runs contrary to the traditional doctrine of God's simplicity (absolute indivisibility) held by Augustine, Anselm, Aquinas and bequeathed to modern evangelicals through the Reformers. As Augustine put it, "Neither does His attention pass from thought to thought, for His knowledge embraces everything in a single spiritual contuition."[4] If God is simple, then his thoughts are not sequential but simultaneous. He does not know things inferentially but intuitively.[5] If God is not simple, then he would think in temporal succession. And, if God is temporal then he is also spatial.[6] Indeed, such a God would even be material (which is contrary to Scripture, e.g., Jn 4:24). And if God is limited to the space-time world then he could think no faster than the speed of light.[7] Thus he would not even be able to know the whole universe at a given moment, to say nothing of having an infallible knowledge of the future. Furthermore, if God is so limited, then he is subject to disorder and to entropy (that is, running out of usable energy).

There are many problems for a process theology, but a process view of God is neither necessary nor helpful. Such a view lacks biblical foundation. The God of the Bible knows everything, including the end from the beginning (Is 46:10). He is a God who cannot change (Mal 3:6), not even in the slightest (Jas 1:17).

Predetermination is in spite of God's foreknowledge. Another possible way to relate divine sovereignty and human freedom is to hold that God

---

[4]Augustine *City of God* 11.21. See other select passages by Augustine in *What St. Augustine Says*, ed. Norman L. Geisler (Grand Rapids, Mich.: Baker, 1982), chap. 3.
[5]Thomas Aquinas *Summa Theologiae* 1.14.7. Trans. by Thomas Gornall (New York: McGraw-Hill Book Co., 1964), 4:27-28.
[6]Paul Helm, "God and Spacelessness," *Philosophy* 55:212 (March 1980): 211-21.
[7]See the excellent critique of process theology by Royce Gruenler, *The Inexhaustible God: Biblical Faith and the Challenge of Process Theism* (Grand Rapids, Mich.: Baker, 1983).

operates with such unapproachable sovereignty that his choices are
made with total disregard for human choices. For example, God determines to save whomever he wishes regardless of whether they chose to
believe or not.

There is an important corollary to this view. If free choices were not
considered at all when God made the list of the elect, then irresistible
grace on the unwilling follows. Humans would have no say in their
salvation. Accordingly, the fact that some (even all) do not choose to
love, worship and serve God will make no difference whatsoever to
God. He will simply doublewhammy them with his irresistible power and
bring them screaming and kicking into his kingdom against their
will. Both the later Augustine and Calvin seemed to have held this view.
Since Augustine believed that heretics could be coerced to believe
against their free choice, he saw no problem in God's doing the same
for the elect.[8]

There are several problems with this position. First, it involves a
denial of free choice. As Augustine himself stated earlier, "he that is
willing is free from compulsion."[9] In the final analysis, humans have
no choice in their own salvation. As Jonathan Edwards held, "free
choice" is doing what we desire, but it is God who gives the desire. But
since God only gives the desire to some (not all), this leads to another
problem. Irresistible grace (?) on the unwilling is a violation of free
choice. For true love is persuasive but never coercive. There can be no
shotgun weddings in heaven. God is not a cosmic B. F. Skinner who
behaviorally modifies humans against their will.[10] Despite an unfortu-
nate metaphor about his own conversion (in which he claims to have
been brought "screaming and kicking into the kingdom"), C. S. Lewis
has two of the finest passages in print against irresistible force used on
unwilling unbelievers. In *The Screwtape Letters* Lewis concludes that
"the Irresistible and the Indisputable are the two weapons which the
very nature of His [God's] scheme forbids Him to use. Merely to
override a human will . . . would be for Him useless. He cannot ravish.

---

[8]Geisler, *What Augustine Says,* chap. 7.
[9]Ibid., p. 158 (from *Two Souls Against the Manicheans* 10.14).
[10]See Norman L. Geisler, "Human Destiny: Free or Forced?" *Christian Scholar's Review*
9, no. 2 (1979): 99-100.

He can only woo."[11] In *The Great Divorce* Lewis shows how God will ultimately respect the free choice with which he has endowed his creatures: "There are only two kinds of people in the end: those who say to God, 'Thy will be done,' and those to whom God says, in the end, 'Thy will be done.' All that are in Hell, choose it. Without that self-choice there could be no Hell."[12]

In spite of some apparent inconsistency on this point (compare his comments on Lk 14:23), John Calvin faces honestly the biblical teaching that the Holy Spirit can be resisted. Stephen said of the Jews, "You stiff-necked people, with uncircumcised hearts and ears! You are just like your fathers: You always resist the Holy Spirit!" (Acts 7:51). Commenting on this passage Calvin said, "Finally, they are said to be resisting the Spirit, when they stubbornly reject what He says by the prophets."[13] Calvin describes this resistance by phrases such as, "stubbornly reject," "intentionally rebel" and "wage war on God."

Irresistible force used by God on his free creatures would be a violation of both the charity of God and the dignity of humans. God is love. True love never forces itself on anyone. Forced love is rape, and God is not a divine rapist![14]

Second, logically this view seems to lead to a denial of God's omnibenevolence (all-lovingness). The Bible says "God is love" (1 Jn 4:16) and that he "loves the world" (Jn 3:16). In fact, "God does not show favoritism" (Rom 2:11), not only in his justice but in all his attributes including love (Mt 5:45). In fact, if God is simple, then his love extends to all his essence, not just part of it. Hence, God cannot be partly loving. But if God is all-loving, then how can he love only some so as to give them and only them the desire to be saved?

Suppose a farmer discovers three boys drowning in his pond where signs clearly forbid swimming. Further, noting their clear disobedience, he says to himself, "They have violated the warning and have brought these deserved consequences on themselves." Thus far we may

---

[11]C. S. Lewis, *The Screwtape Letters* (New York: Macmillan, 1961), p. 38.

[12]C. S. Lewis, *The Great Divorce* (New York: Macmillan, 1945), p. 69.

[13]John Calvin, *Calvin's New Testament Commentaries,* trans. A. W. Morrison (Grand Rapids, Mich.: Eerdmans, 1972), 6:213.

[14]Norman L. Geisler, *The Roots of Evil* (Grand Rapids, Mich.: Zondervan, 1978), pp. 85-88.

be willing to agree. But if the farmer proceeds to say, "Therefore I will make no attempt to rescue them," we would immediately think something is lacking in his love. And suppose by some inexplicable whim he should declare "I have no obligation to save any of them, but out of the goodness of my heart I will save one of them and let the other two drown." In such a case we would surely consider his love partial.

Certainly this is not the picture we find of the God of the Bible who "loved the world" (Jn 3:16), sent his Son to be a sacrifice not only for our sins "but also for the sins of the whole world" (1 Jn 2:2) and whose Son "died for the ungodly" (not just for the elect). Indeed, the God of the Bible "wants all men to be saved and to come to a knowledge of the truth" (1 Tim 2:4). Peter even speaks of those "denying the sovereign Lord who bought them" (2 Pet 2:1).

Even John Calvin believed the Christ died for all the sins of the world (Col 1:15) by which he clearly meant "the salvation of the human race."[15] Commenting on the "many" for whom Christ died in Mark 14:24, Calvin said, "the word many does not mean a part of the world only, but the whole human race."[16]

God's predetermination is in accord with his foreknowledge. There is a third way of relating divine sovereignty and human freedom. Perhaps God's predetermination is neither *based on* his foreknowledge of human free choices nor done *in spite of* it. The Scriptures, for example, declare that we are "chosen *according to* the foreknowledge of God" (1 Pet 1:2). That is to say, there is no chronological or logical priority of election and foreknowledge. As a simple Being, all of God's attributes are one with his indivisible essence. Hence, both foreknowledge and predetermination are one in God. Thus whatever God knows, he determines. And whatever he determines, he knows.

More properly, we should speak of God as *knowingly determining* and *determinately knowing* from all eternity everything that happens, including all free acts. As John Walvoord insightfully commented on 1 Peter 1:2, it "teaches not the logical order of election in relation to foreknowledge by the fact that they are coextensive." In other words, all

---

[15]John Calvin *Institutes of Christian Religion* 3.1.1.
[16]Calvin, *Calvin's New Testament Commentaries*, 3:139. See also Calvin's comments on John 1:29, Romans 5:15; 1 John 2:2.

aspects of the eternal purpose of God are equally timeless.[17] For if God is an eternal and simple Being then his thoughts must be coordinate and unified.

Whatever he forechooses cannot be *based on* what he foreknows. Nor can what he foreknows be based on what he *forechose*. Both must be simultaneous and coordinate acts of God. Thus God knowingly determined and determinately knew from all eternity everything that would come to pass, including all free acts. Hence, there are truly free actions, and God determined they would be such. God then is totally sovereign in the sense of actually determining what occurs, and yet humans are completely free and responsible for what they choose.

Determinism and Free Choice

Granting the foregoing conclusion, one of the most persistent philosophical problems is the alleged contradiction in God's infallibly foreknowing events which humans freely perform. The argument can be stated as follows:

1. Whatever an all-knowing God foreknows about the future must come to pass (otherwise he would be wrong in what he knows).

2. God foreknew that Judas would betray Christ.

3. Therefore, Judas must betray Christ. (If he did not, then God would have been wrong in what he foreknew.)

4. But if Judas must betray Christ, then he was not free not to betray him (since free choice implies that he could have done otherwise).

5. Therefore, if God foreknows the future, then the future is not free (or vice versa).

Historically, Christians have always affirmed the truth of the first premise that God knows everything, including the whole future of the universe. Recently, under the devastating influence of process theology, some theologians have ventured beyond the bounds of historic orthodoxy into the radical suggestion that God may not know all future acts with absolute certainty. But this view would mean, as one process thinker boldly admitted, that "God is watching with bated breath."[18]

---

[17]Lewis Sperry Chafer and John Walvoord, *Major Bible Themes* (Grand Rapids, Mich.: Zondervan, 1980), p. 233.

[18]See Bernard Loomer, "A Response to David Griffin," *Encounter* 36, no. 4 (Autumn 1975): 365.

The second premise is also granted by biblical theology. God knows "the end from the beginning" (Is 46:10). And Jesus knew in advance that Judas would betray him as the Scriptures had said (Jn 13:2; Acts 1:20).

What many people do not fully appreciate is that premise 4 follows logically from the first three. If God cannot be wrong about what he knows and if he knows Judas will betray Christ, then it cannot be any other way—Judas must betray Christ. If Judas had decided not to betray Christ, then God would have been wrong.

Premise 5, however, does not follow logically from the first four premises. It is not necessary to grant that Judas was not free in his betrayal of Christ. First, the fact that the act of betrayal was necessary from the standpoint of God's knowledge does not mean it was not free from Judas's vantage point. As Aquinas noted, "things known by God are contingent because of their contingent causes [free choices], though the first cause, God's knowledge, is necessary."[19]

The *Westminster Confession* (1646) makes this point well when it says: "Although in relation to the foreknowledge and decree of God, the first cause, all things come to pass immutably and infallibly, yet by the same providence he ordereth them to fall out, according to the nature of the second causes, either necessarily, freely, or contingently."[20]

In brief, God *determined* that Judas would *freely* betray Christ. There is no logical contradiction between determinism and free will. There would be a contradiction only if God *forced* Judas to *freely* betray Christ. Forced freedom is a contradiction in terms. But if God simply determines that Judas will *freely* do it, then there is no contradiction. God can determine through free choice with the same certainty that he can determine without it. An omniscient mind cannot be wrong.

Second, simply because something is determined does not mean that what happened was not free. The events of the past are determined; they cannot be changed. Yet we recognize that many of them resulted from free choices. For example, yesterday I freely chose to listen to some music (which I seldom listen to). But now that this is in the past,

---

[19]Thomas Aquinas *Summa Theologiae* 1.14.13, Reply 1. Also Loomer, "Response to Griffin."

[20]*The Westminster Confession* (1646; reprint ed., Atlanta: John Knox Press, 1963), 5.2.200.

I can no longer choose not to do it. It is forever determined. Never-theless, when I did it I was completely free. Hence, there is no con-tradiction between an event resulting from a totally free choice and at the same time being completely determined. But if God is all-knowing, then he can know the future with the same certainty that he can know the past. Thus the future can be absolutely determined and yet some events can be totally free.

Third, in a more precise sense there is no problem of God's fore-knowledge predetermining events. Since God is an eternal being, he does not really foreknow anything. He simply *knows* eternally. Until recent high-risk diversions into process thought by a few thinkers on the fringe of the movement, orthodox Christians from Augustine through C. S. Lewis have stoutly maintained that God is an eternal, nontemporal being.[21] Despite the many anthropomorphisms picturing God in temporal terms, God's nontemporal nature is supported by numerous passages of Scripture (for example, Ex 3:14; Jn 8:58). As Jude put it, God is "before all ages" (v. 25). Indeed, Hebrews declares that God "created this world of time" (1:2 Knox).

But granting that God does not pass through temporal successions, then what he thinks, he has forever thought. His thought is perfect and absolute; it needs no progress or improvement. So from God's vantage point he simply knows (not foreknows) what we *are* doing with our free choices. For what we have, are and will choose is *present* to God in his eternal NOW.[22] This being the case, there is no problem of how an act can be truly free if God has determined in advance what will take place. God's foreknowledge is not foreordaining anything which will *later* occur to him. All of time is present to God's mind from all eternity. God does not really foreknow it; he simply knows it in his eternal presence. Hence, God is not foreordaining from his vantage point, but simply ordaining what humans are doing freely. God *sees* what we are freely doing. And what he sees, he knows. And what he knows, he determines. So God *determinately* knows and *knowingly de-termines* what we are freely deciding.

---

[21]See Norman L. Geisler, "Process Theology and Inerrancy," in *Challenges to Inerrancy: A Theological Response,* ed. Gordon Lewis and Bruce Demarest (Chicago: Moody, 1984), pp. 247-84.
[22]Augustine *Confessions* 11.6-27. See also Geisler, "Process Theology," pp. 57-70.

Further, it is not determinism which is contrary to free choice; it is coercion. It is not foreknowledge which eliminates free will but force. Necessity and freedom are not incompatible, but irresistibility and human responsibility are.

The Nature of Free Choice

Thus far we have implied but not explicated what is meant by free choice. A lot of confusion can be avoided by clearly defining what is meant by this important concept. First, let us outline the three major views: moral indeterminism, moral determinism and moral self-determinism. By these we simply mean that a given human moral act is either uncaused, caused by another or caused by oneself.

We shall first examine moral indeterminism. When *indeterminism* is properly defined, it becomes difficult to assert that moral actions are really indeterminate; that is, that they have no efficient cause. It is a fundamental belief of rational thought that every event has an adequate cause. Things do not happen willy-nilly. It is contrary to uniform observation to believe that things pop into existence spontaneously with no necessary and sufficient conditions. Even the skeptic David Hume never denied the principle of causality.[23]

If indeterminism were true, then there would be events without causes. The universe would be irrational and unlivable. In fact, it would be nonmoral since there would be no way to determine who is responsible for an action which has no efficient cause.

Some have mistakenly taken Heisenberg's "principle of indeterminacy" as support for the view described here as indeterminism. Heisenberg's principle states that a subatomic particle has either a precise position or a precise velocity, but not both at the same time. One is indeterminate when the other is determined.

Drawing philosophical conclusions from Heisenberg's work is inappropriate for at least two reasons. Heisenberg's principle describes the subatomic realm which is not known without investigator interference. The instruments by which the subatomic realm is observed bombard the subatomic particles in order to "see" them. Hence, the unpredict-

---

[23]David Hume, *The Letters of David Hume*, ed. J. Y. T. Greig (Oxford: Clarendon Press, 1932), 1:187.

able behavior may result in part from the very attempt to observe them.

Moreover, Heisenberg's principle does not say there is no cause of the events but simply that we cannot predict where a given particle will be at a given time. Hence, it is not to be understood as the principle of uncausality but the principle of unpredictability. And even though a particle's position cannot be predicted, nonetheless the overall pattern can be predicted. At any rate, there is no scientific evidence to support a belief that the events or patterns in the subatomic realm are without a cause. Furthermore, even if there were such evidence, this would not in itself justify extending this "indeterminacy" from the (subatomic) physical realm to the moral realm. By definition, physics deals with what *is* and morality with what *ought* to be.

The second possible way to understand free choice is moral determinism. According to this view, an individual is not the efficient cause of a moral action. In a theistic context, the ultimate cause would be God. The human agent, then, would at best be only an *instrumental* cause (through which the causality flows) not the *efficient* cause (by which the causality is effected).

This view raises serious problems for a Christian. Nonetheless, forms of this position have been espoused by some significant thinkers from Jonathan Edwards to Gordon Clark. The first problem is that logically it makes God the efficient cause of all free choices including evil actions. If individual human agents are not the real efficient causes of evil, then God performs the rapes, murders and other cruelties through humans. This view is biblically unsound and morally repugnant.

Second, this view of freedom eliminates all real moral responsibility. On this view, humans are not efficient causes of their actions but only instruments. Thus, for example, a person performing a murder could not be blamed any more than the gun or the knife (which are instruments of the killing). Similarly, one cannot rationally charge the car of a reckless driver with a crime because it was only the instrument that did the damage. The driver is responsible. In short, moral determinism makes God immoral and makes humans amoral.

The final view of free choice is moral self-determinism. On this view, moral acts are not uncaused or caused by someone else. Rather, they are caused by oneself. This view best fits both the biblical and rational criteria. God said to Eve, "What is this *you* have done?" (Gen 3:13). Even for choices made after the Fall Jesus held the Jews responsible for their condemnation because "*you* were not willing" (Mt 23:37). This is the way it is both throughout Scripture and in everyday life.

Let us briefly consider problems which have been raised against this view. There are several philosophical objections. The first has to do with the principle of causality—that *every* event has an adequate cause. If this is so, then it would seem that even one's free will has a prior cause. If one's free will has a prior cause, then it cannot be caused by oneself. Thus self-determinism would be contrary to the principle of causality which it embraces.

There is a basic confusion in this objection. This confusion results in part from an infelicitous expression of the self-determinism view. Representatives of moral self-determinism sometimes speak of free will as though it were the efficient cause of moral actions. This would lead one naturally to ask: What is the cause of one's free will? But a more precise description of the process of a free act would avoid this problem. Technically, free will is not the efficient cause of a free act; free will is simply the power through which the agent performs the free act. The efficient cause of the free act is really the free *agent*, not the free will. Free will is simply the power by which the free agent acts. We do not say that humans *are* free will but only that they *have* free will. Likewise, we do not say that humans are thought but only that they have the power of thought. So it is not the power of free choice which causes a free act, but the *person* who has this power.

Now if the real cause of a free act is not an act but an *actor*, then it makes no sense to ask for the cause of the actor as though the actor were another act. The cause of a performance is the performer. It is meaningless to ask what performance caused the performance. Likewise, the cause of a free act is not another free act. Rather, it is a free agent. And once we have arrived at the free agent, it is meaningless to ask what caused its free acts. For if something else caused its actions, then the agent is not the cause of them and thus is not responsible for them. The free moral agent is the cause of free moral actions. And it is as senseless to ask what caused the free agent to act as it is to ask who made God? The answer is the same in both instances: nothing can cause the first cause because it is the first. There is nothing before the first. Likewise, humans are the first cause of their own moral actions. If humans were not the first cause of their own free actions, then the actions would not be *their* actions.

If it is argued that it is impossible to claim that humans can be the first cause of their moral actions, then it is also impossible for God to be the first cause of his moral actions. Tracing the first cause of human actions back to God does not solve the problem of finding a cause for every action. It simply pushes the problem back farther. Sooner or later theists will have to admit that a free act is a self-determined act which is not caused by another. Eventually it must be acknowledged that all acts come from actors, but that actors (free agents) are the first cause of their actions which therefore have no prior cause.

The real question, then, is not whether there are agents who cause their own actions but whether God is the only true agent (that is, person) in the universe. Christians have always denounced (as pantheism) the belief that there is ultimately only one agent (or person) in the universe. But the denial of human free agency is reducible to this charge.

There is a second philosophical problem with the claim that humans are the first cause of their own actions: It violates the principle of causality. If we say that a human agent's actions are not caused then have we not admitted that there are uncaused events in the universe? This charge is based on a misunderstanding of the difference between uncaused and self-caused actions. Moral self-determinists do not claim there are any uncaused moral actions. They in fact believe all moral actions are caused by moral agents. But unlike the moral determinist who believes all human acts are caused by another (for example, by God), self-determinists believe that there are more agents than God. Nonetheless, self-determinists believe that there is a cause for every moral action and that the cause is a moral agent, whether it is God or some moral creature.

But does not this conclusion lead to a third problem? Are not self-determined actions self-caused? And is it not impossible to cause oneself? Here again there is a confusion of act and actor. No actor (agent) can cause itself to exist. A cause is (in its being) prior to its effect. But one cannot be prior to oneself. A self-caused *being* (actor) is impossible. But a self-caused *action* is not impossible, since the actor (cause) must be prior to its action (effect). So self-caused *being* is impossible, but self-caused *becoming* is not. We determine what we will become morally. But only God determines what we are. So, while persons cannot cause their own being, they can cause their own behavior.

Perhaps some of the confusion here could be cleared away if we did not speak of self-determinism, as though we were determining our own *selves*. Moral self-determinism does not refer to the determination *of* oneself but determination *by* oneself. So it would be more proper not to speak of self-caused action but of an action caused by oneself. But even without this distinction, there is a significant difference between a self-caused being and a self-caused action. The former is clearly impossible while the latter is not. A being cannot be prior to itself, but an actor must be prior to its act.

The fourth philosophical problem with a self-deterministic view of freedom is this: How can God determine the future without violating free choice? One of the difficulties with holding to a strong determinism (wherein God infallibly knows and determines all that comes to pass) lies in just how God can do this. It is not difficult to understand how God can bring about a necessary end through necessary means (such as determining in advance that the last domino in a falling series will drop too). But how can God bring about a necessary end through contingent means (such as free choice)?

Typically those who hold this view simply plead mystery. There certainly is a mystery here, but it may be helpful to explain *what* a mystery is and *why* this situation is a mystery. Following the traditional distinction, we take a mystery to be something that is not *contrary* to reason, but which goes *beyond* reason. By this we mean that the two truths (God's sovereignty and human free choice) are noncontradictory but incomprehensible. We can apprehend both truths but we cannot comprehend how they relate. We know that both are true, but we do not know how this is so.

Now that we have described what is meant by the mystery of human free will and divine determinism, just why is it a mystery? Or, to put it another way, why is it that we cannot know how the two fit together? Why cannot we know *how* God determines free actions without violating their freedom? I would suggest that the reason we cannot know how is because there is no "how" to be known. "How" questions imply a mechanism, a modus operandi or an intermediate force. But if the interaction between sovereignty and free choice is immediate, then there is no intermediate means.

By the very nature of the case there is no intermediate means between God (the primary efficient cause) and humans (the secondary efficient causes) of free actions. God is the cause of the fact of freedom, and humans are the causes of the acts of freedom. God made the agent, but the agents cause the actions. God gives people power (of free choice), but they exercise it without coercion. Thus God is responsible for bestowing freedom, but humans are responsible for behaving with it.

This view could be called "soft" determinism in contrast to "hard" determinism. The latter holds that God not only gives humans the power of free choice, but God actually performs the free choice through humans. In "hard" determinism, the free agents are really only instrumental causes, not efficient causes of their own action. God both caused the fact of human freedom and he actually performs the acts of human freedom. In short, humans are not human, they are puppets or robots.

But to return to the main point: If there is no intermediate cause between God's determination and human free choice, then the "how" question evaporates. The only answer to how God did it is *by his infinite power and wisdom.* Why (final cause) God did it may be answerable (for example, for his glory), but how he did it is answerable only by his direct power and knowledge (efficient cause) and not by any other means (instrumental cause). For there is no instrumental cause between God's sovereign will and human free will. The former acts on the latter directly from all eternity. Although God acts in time he nonetheless acts from eternity. That is, God acted from eternity even though the results of his actions occur in the world at different times. As the doctor makes one decision that the patient should take a pill each day for fourteen days, so God decreed simultaneously from all eternity what takes place sequentially throughout time.

There is also a biblical problem with the moral self-determinism view. How can salvation be all of grace if it is dependent on our free choices? The Bible teaches that all the regenerate (justified) will ultimately be saved (Rom 8:29). None shall perish (Jn 10:26-30) or ever be separated from Christ (Rom 8:36-39). Indeed, all believers are in

Christ (2 Cor 5:17; Eph 1:4) and are part of his body (1 Cor 12:13). Hence, if any were severed from Christ, then Christ would have to be severed from himself! Humans can be faithless to God, but God cannot deny himself (2 Tim 2:13). Salvation is not dependent on humans but on God. Hence, it cannot be lost. Salvation was not gained by human will (Jn 1:13; Rom 9:16) and, therefore, it is not of works, lest anyone should boast (Eph 2:8-9).

But if salvation is conditioned wholly on God's grace and not on our will, then how can our free choices play any part in our salvation? The answer to this question is found in an important distinction between two senses of the word *condition*. There are no conditions for God's giving salvation; it is wholly of grace. But there is one (and only one) condition for receiving this gift—true saving faith.

There is absolutely nothing in humans which is the basis for God's saving us. But there was something in God (love) which is the basis for human salvation. It was not because of any merit but only because of grace that salvation was initiated toward us. We do not initiate salvation (Rom 3:11), and we cannot attain it. But we can and must receive it (Jn 1:12). Salvation is an unconditional act of God's election. Our faith is not a condition for God's giving salvation, but it is for our receiving it. Nonetheless, the act of faith (free choice) by which we receive salvation is not meritorious. It is the giver who gets credit for the gift, not the receiver.

Practical Application

A psychology teacher once wisely remarked that a good theory is a very practical thing. So it is with good theology. Good doctrines give rise to good deeds. Hence, a proper understanding of divine sovereignty will serve as the basis for a proper understanding of human responsibility. Now let us relate this to the illustration about Fred.

Fred's Case. First of all, Fred should recognize that all that he has is a gift from God. "Every good and perfect gift is from above, coming down from the Father of the heavenly lights" (Jas 1:17). As Job said, "Naked I came from my mother's womb, and naked I will depart" (Job 1:21).

Second, Fred should be grateful for what he has. "Give thanks in all circumstances, for this is God's will for you in Christ Jesus" (1 Thess

5:18). This includes thanks for daily food, clothes and shelter (1 Tim 6:8). Indeed, the Bible speaks of food "which God created to be received with thanksgiving by those who believe and who know the truth" (1 Tim 4:3). And riches themselves are a gift of God (Eccles 5:19).

Third, since God "richly provides us with everything for our enjoyment" (1 Tim 6:17), Fred should enjoy what God gave him. God is not a Heavenly Scrooge or Cosmic Killjoy. He wants us to enjoy life. Indeed, "no good thing does he withhold from those whose walk is blameless" (Ps 84:11). Over and over, Ecclesiastes commands us to "eat and drink and find satisfaction in [our] work" (2:24, compare 3:13; 5:19; 8:15). The fact that some are hungry should not keep the unselfish from enjoying food. Pain should not be able to veto all pleasure.

Fourth, Fred should share what he has with those who do not have. Proverbs says "a generous man will himself be blessed, for he shares his food with the poor" (22:9). Paul added for the rich, "Command them to do good, to be rich in good deeds, and to be generous and willing to share" (1 Tim 6:18). The early church was careful to "remember the poor" (Gal 2:10). For, as John reminds us, "if anyone has material possessions and sees his brother in need but has no pity on him, how can the love of God be in him?" (1 Jn 3:17). Indeed, Jesus said, "whatever you did for one of the least of these [the poor, hungry, naked, imprisoned] brothers of mine, you did for me" (Mt 25:40).

Fred should remember that God sovereignly gave us the human responsibility of helping others. The obligation to perform acts of love is a sovereignly determined one. As Paul said in Ephesians, God "chose [elected] us . . . to be holy and blameless in his sight" (Eph 1:4). We are "predestined to be conformed to the likeness of his Son" (Rom 8:29). There is a practical purpose for predestination. God chose us to be conveyers, not mere containers, of his riches whether material or spiritual (2 Cor 4:7). On the other hand, there is no sin in being rich. Many great men of God (including Abraham, Job and Solomon) were very rich. There is nothing wrong with possessing possessions. It is being possessed by them that is a sin. For "a man's life does not consist in the abundance of his possessions" (Lk 12:15).

In short, Fred should recognize that a sovereign and gracious God has blessed him with riches. He should be thankful for them, enjoy them and recognize his moral obligation to share them with those in need. On the other hand, the poor should be content in what they have (Phil 4:11). They should not covet or steal their neighbor's goods (Ex 20:15). They should work hard to improve their lot (1 Thess 4:11-12). But they must also recognize that God in his sovereignty has graciously allotted to each as he will gifts both spiritual (1 Cor 12:21-22) and material (Eccles 5:19).

The poor should also be thankful for they are specially blessed with riches in spirit (Lk 6:20). And God has saved them from the temptation of riches (1 Tim 6:9). Thus they should recognize that "godliness with contentment is great gain" (1 Tim 6:6).

Prescriptively, we should work to alleviate the needs of the poor. But descriptively, as Jesus said, "the poor you will always have with you" (Mt 26:11). Not until Christ returns will everyone have "his own vine and fig tree" (Is 36:16).

Mary's Case. The *will of God* is a troublesome phrase primarily because it is loaded with ambiguity. In one sense everything happens in accord with God's will, namely, the sovereign decree by which he rules the universe. In another sense, every sin is contrary to God's will, namely, his command for creaturely conduct. Similarly, in one sense God wills only the salvation of the elect for only they have been chosen in Christ according to "the purpose of his will" (Eph 1:11). Yet in another sense of the term, God is "not willing that any should perish" (2 Pet 3:9 KJV).

In short, there is a difference between what God decrees and what he desires. He decrees everything, both good and evil. But God desires only good. So God desired the very best for Mary. He desired that she study hard (Mt 22:36-37), that she reach her fullest potential, and that she maximize her talents for his glory (1 Cor 10:31; Phil 1:10). However, Mary's failure to do this did not catch God by surprise. God knows our uprisings and downfallings. He is not dependent on us, and he is not waiting with bated breath to see what we will do. In fact, he has planned our failures into his overall program of success from all eternity. For "surely the wrath of man shall praise [God]" (Ps 76:10 KJV).

There are three different aspects of the will of God spelled out in the Bible: God's prescriptive will, God's permissive will and God's providential will. All of these are part of his sovereign will (decree) for the universe.

First we have God's prescriptive will. God promised Abraham and his offspring the land of Canaan for an inheritance (Gen 12). He commanded them to dwell in the land and to claim it for their inheritance. In accordance with this God commanded Isaac: "Do not go down to Egypt" (Gen 26:2). This was God's *prescriptive* will. It is what he desired for them. This prescriptive sense of God's will involves only good. For God is so holy that he cannot even look on evil approvingly (Hab 1:13).

It is only in the permissive sense of God's will that he allows some evil. Abraham and his descendants failed God under testing (famine) and departed the land of promise for "greener" pastures in Egypt. God permitted this but did not prescribe it. God commands only good, but he concedes to evil. God never encourages evil, though he does allow it. So, eventually God said to Jacob: "Go now to Egypt." This he said, not because it was God's perfect will or permanent desire, but because it was his permissive will for the time being in order to accomplish his ultimate goal for their lives. As Jesus said, "Moses permitted you to divorce your wives because your hearts were hard" (Mt 19:8). Not that it was in accord with God's ideal will, but that it was his accommodation to our stubborn will.

Finally, we have God's providential will. In spite of Israel's failure to claim and live in the land, God's sovereign purposes for them could not be frustrated. God's prescriptive will was that they not go to Egypt. His permissive will was to allow them to go to Egypt. But eventually God's providential will was accomplished when he declared: "Out of Egypt I called my son" (Hos 11:1).

In like manner God's prescriptive will for our lives is not to sin. Yet God's permissive will is to allow sin, so that in his providential will he can bring good even out of our sin. As Joseph said to his brothers, "you intended to harm me, but God intended it for good" (Gen 50:20). "Where sin increased, grace increased all the more" (Rom 5:20). Nevertheless, God forbid that we should sin. We should not prescribe beating one's head against the wall because it will feel so good when one stops. But we should permit the pain of the dentist's chair so that the tooth will be better as a result.

We may conclude that in the prescriptive sense of God's will, Mary should have been obedient to every command of Scripture for her, including those for diligent use of her talents (Mt 25:28) and time (Col 4:5) for God. In this sense she could have missed God's best for her life, even though what she did was good. It is wrong, however, to sacrifice the best on the altar of the good. She is accountable for her free choice in the matter, for God only sovereignly willed to permit her to do what is evil. Her acts were self-determined, and God cannot be blamed for her wrong choices in life (assuming that she should have been a doctor).

On the other hand, God is gracious and forgiving, and Mary need not go through life with guilt and a sense of uselessness. God can literally redeem her life in his gracious providence and make her a good and useful nurse. In fact, as bones grow stronger after a break, so believers can be more mature after God has allowed them to drift from his prescriptive will. Thus God in his providence can sometimes even "repay . . . for the years the locusts have eaten" (Joel 2:25) while one was in his permissive will. But never for even a moment can anything in the universe move outside his sovereign will. God has determined everything (even our free choices) and his ultimate purposes cannot be frustrated.

John Feinberg's Response

AS I READ NORMAN GEISLER'S PRESENTATION, I AM PLEASED WITH HIS strong position on the sovereignty of God. Likewise, I find myself in virtual agreement with his first few pages. Nonetheless, I find his overall presentation to be extremely problematic. There are problems with the way he presents the options on such issues as the nature of free choice and the relation of determinism to foreknowledge in that he appears to present a caricature of views other than his own. For example, what indeterminist would describe his position as Geisler presents it on pages 74-75? Likewise, his handling of how God knows the future basically adopts the problematic Boethian answer. Nonetheless, there are two major problems that are crucial to our discussion, and I shall focus on them.

The first major problem stems from a claim which initially appears quite harmless until we see what Geisler does with it. Geisler claims that because God is simple, his thoughts are not sequential but simultaneous (p. 68). Geisler later applies this notion to the relation of foreknowledge to predetermination. He writes, "That is to say, there is no chronological or logical priority of election and foreknowledge. As a simple Being, all of God's attributes are one with his indivisible essence" (p. 70). This is Geisler's answer to the problem of the relation of God's foreordination to his foreknowledge. Rather than saying God foreordains what he foreknows (as many Arminians say) or that God foreknows because he foreordains (as many Calvinists say) Geisler chooses neither option. He argues on the basis of God's simplicity that foreknowledge and foreordination are simultaneous, equally timeless, because God is eternal. Neither is temporally or even *logically* prior to the other. There are several problems with this view.

Geisler's fundamental problem stems from his understanding of God's attributes as they relate to his actions. To say that God is simple means that his *being* is not divisible into parts. But God's thoughts and mental acts such as decreeing, foreknowing and so on are *not* part of his essence or attributes any more than his acts in the world, such as creating or preserving the universe, are part of his essence or attributes. Geisler treats God's thoughts as part of his essence and/or attributes, and since God's essence is simple, Geisler concludes that God's thoughts must not be distinguishable into sequential parts. That is a mistake of the first order!

In assessing Geisler's views I can agree that whatever God knows, he knows all at once and has always known, and I agree that God foreordained all things at once. However, such things are true of God not in virtue of his simplicity but in virtue of his omniscience and sovereign will. But, granting God such knowledge does *not* mean that he does not know the logical sequence and relations among the items that he knows. Moreover, granting that God foreordains all things simultaneously does not mean that there is no logical order in what he foreordains. For example, God always knew that Christ would be born and would also die. But he also understood that logically (as well as chronologically) one of those events had to precede the other. That does not mean that God knew one of those events before he knew the other. It only means that in *knowing* both simultaneously, he knows the logical and chronological relation between the two events. Moreover, God foreordained both events simultaneously, but that does not mean he did not recognize the logical point that no one can be foreordained to die who has not been foreordained to be born. Making such claims as I have only eliminates the simplicity of God if one confuses his being and attributes with his acts (mental).

Let us apply the above to the problem at hand. If one grants that God's act of foreknowing does not *temporally* precede his act of foreordaining, one can still ask about the *logical* relation between God's acts of foreknowing and foreordaining without eliminating anything about the simplicity of God. In other words, it is still legitimate and most important to know whether God chooses because of what he foresees or whether he foresees because he has foreordained. Geisler seems to reject the former option but does not answer in terms of the latter. In fact, Geisler refuses to answer the question, because he argues that it will commit him to saying there is a sequence in God's thoughts which he thinks eliminates God's simplicity. However, once one recognizes the error in confusing God's acts with his attributes, there should be no hesitation to answer the question. Geisler never answers the question, even though it is crucial to the whole understanding of God's sovereignty as it relates to human freedom. Consequently, his discussion on the relation of foreknowledge to determinism resolves nothing and leaves us to wonder whether he is an Arminian/indeterminist or a Calvinist/determinist.

A second major problem concerns Geisler's notion of freedom. Geisler opts for what he calls self-determinism, but the view resolves nothing in the debate between determinism and indeterminism. The basic problem is a refusal to address a key issue, and that stems from a refusal to answer two separate questions. Put simply, one must answer both of the following: (1) what is the cause of an act? (2) what is it that causes the agent to act? Geisler's whole discussion focuses on the first question, but ignores the second. Geisler argues long and hard that it is the agent who causes the act, but surely most determinists and all indeterminists would agree, for the point seems almost self-evidently true that if I act, I am the cause of my action. However, focusing on that issue alone does not explain why determinists and indeterminists who agree with him on that point still disagree with one another on the notion of freedom. The answer is that they answer the second question differently. The indeterminist argues that what causes the agent to act is nothing which decisively inclines the will. The determinist argues the opposite. Geisler rejects the question (pp. 76-78).

Despite Geisler's claims, the question is not nonsensical, and it is critical to this whole issue of divine sovereignty and human freedom. It is not nonsensical, because if one points out what led the agent to decide as she did, that does not mean someone else or something else *did* the act. The act is still the act of the agent! It is crucial to our discussion, for without an answer to that question it is impossible to say how God's sovereignty relates to human freedom. Does God sovereignly bring it about that we do determinedly but unconstrainedly what God has foreordained? Does he bring it about that we constrainedly do his bidding? Or does he refuse to exert his power to ensure that we choose one thing or another? Without an answer to those questions, we do not know what a theologian thinks about the nature of human freedom or the relation of God's sovereignty to that freedom. Geisler, in rejecting such questions by focusing on the cause of the act apart from what causes the agent to act, essentially refuses to answer the main issue under discussion in this book. In this volume we are offered three answers. Each is possible, regardless of which is accepted. But, since each is a possible answer, there is no need to conclude as Geisler does that the answer to how God can determine all things and yet maintain human freedom is ultimately a mystery.

In sum, though there are many problematic items in Geisler's presentation, the fundamental difficulty is a refusal to answer two questions: (1) does God foreknow because he foreordains or does he foreordain because he foreknows? (2) does the agent act because of causal factors which decisively incline the will or does he act without any factors decisively inclining the will? Geisler's refusal to answer those questions stems from other problems I have noted. The key point, though, is that without an answer to those questions it is impossible to know how a thinker puts together the sovereignty of God and human freedom. Consequently, even though Geisler's essay is interesting, it is rather unhelpful for resolving anything substantial in regard to the issues before us.

Bruce Reichenbach's Response

NORMAN GEISLER SUGGESTS THAT THE RELATION BETWEEN DIVINE SOV-
ereignty and human freedom is a mystery. In a mystery, he states, we
know two or more truths but cannot comprehend how they fit together.[1] But though their logical consistency is beyond human reason, ultimately (for God) they are consistent.

But are divine sovereignty and human freedom *in the particular way
Geisler understands them* candidates for being a mystery, or are they
really inconsistent? To answer this question, let us first ask what Geisler
means by both of these concepts.

Though he never defines sovereignty, he does characterize it by saying that God *controls* whatever comes to exist and all that happens,
directs the course of events, and *determines* everything that occurs and
effectively works to bring it about. He directly determines human activity; that is, he acts immediately on human persons as the primary
cause of their actions (p. 79).

Geisler characterizes freedom in three ways. A free act is not forced
or coerced. It is an act caused by the agent (it is self-determined). And
it implies that the person could have done otherwise.

---

[1] Geisler does not state whether these two truths *appear* to be inconsistent, though it
would seem that this would be required if we are to have the aura of mystery.

Given these characterizations, we can now ask whether divine sovereignty and human freedom *as Geisler sees them* are really consistent. To explore this, let us take each of these characteristics of freedom and apply them to an example he suggests, that of Judas betraying Jesus. We will begin with Geisler's contention that free acts are self-determined. He claims that Judas's act of betrayal was both determined by God (in that all that occurs is determined by God) and a free act determined by Judas and not by another (self-determined). But this is contradictory. If the act of betrayal is determined by Judas and not by another, it cannot be determined by God, and vice versa.[2]

Furthermore, if a person is free he is able to do otherwise than he does in those cases where he is free. If Judas's treachery was a free act, then Judas could have done otherwise than he did. He could have chosen not to have betrayed Jesus. But since all events are determined by God according to his eternal plan, the act of treachery was necessary and Judas could not have done otherwise than he did, for, as Geisler tells us, God effects his plans with certainty (p. 72). This too is a contradiction. If the act was necessary, it could not have been performed otherwise than it was, and vice versa.

Geisler would reply that it is a contradiction only because we have confused two standpoints, that of Judas and that of God. From Judas's standpoint, the event did not have to occur. Judas could have not betrayed our Lord. From God's standpoint, it was necessary. The treachery was determined by God and could not have been otherwise. But will this work? No, for if Judas could have chosen not to betray Jesus, then the fact that his choice agreed with God's timeless plan was merely a fortunate happenstance for God. Such a view fails to correlate with Geisler's view of divine sovereignty, which sees God as being in control of everything, determining with certainty every outcome. If, on the other hand, the act had to occur, the fact that Judas desired to do it was again a fortunate circumstance. For otherwise presumably God would have had to act in some way to bring it about since it was part of his eternal, divine plan. Given Geisler's position, Judas maintains his

---

[2]Of course, the other two options are likewise unacceptable for him. If it is determined partly by God and partly by Judas, the act is not wholly Judas's, and he is not solely responsible for it but shares that responsibility with God. If it is determined by God, Judas was not free.

freedom to do what he wants only as long as his choices accord with God's plan, which is no freedom at all. He could not have acted in a manner inconsistent with God's determinate plan.

Let us now turn to the characteristic of freedom relating to coercion. The contradiction also arises here, though not so obviously. On the one hand, there is no evidence that Judas was coerced into his betrayal. It was something he freely chose to do. Yet what does Geisler mean when he says that God determined that Judas betray Jesus? Unfortunately Geisler never defines what he means by *determine*. However, in the chapter he equates self-determination with self-causation (pp. 76-78). If this is so, then to determine is to cause, and if God determines that Judas betray Jesus, he causes Judas to betray Jesus and we again have a contradiction. Judas was not coerced to act, yet Judas was caused by God to act as he did.

Here again Geisler might reply that we have misunderstood his position. He might say that our criticism confuses him with what he calls a hard determinist. Later in his chapter he suggests that, according to his soft determinism, God determines in that he creates the agents, but the agents themselves freely choose and cause the action (pp. 78-79).

But this characterization fails to square with his view of divine sovereignty. For if all that God does is make free persons, it makes no sense to say that God determines, controls and directs every action. If agents are free, though God creates and sustains them, what they do is up to them, and this could be something which goes contrary to God's plans and purposes. No, if God determines, controls and directs every action, then the action itself cannot be contrary to what God determines, and as such, it is not the result of a *free* act of the agent.

Geisler suggests that, though our actions are determined by God, they are free because they are willed or desired by us. Judas really wanted to betray Jesus. But this will not rescue his position, for willing or desiring is itself an event. And since all events are controlled and determined by God, the fact that Judas willed or desired money is itself determined or controlled by God. Thus, Judas could not have willed to do other than he did.

In short, if God merely determines that free persons exist, then they can self-determine their actions and are free. God cannot sovereignly control their actions in the sense that he can guarantee with certainty what they will do. If, on the other hand, God sovereignly determines and controls every action, persons cannot do otherwise than they do and they are not free. Geisler's position is not a genuine mystery; it instead involves two contradictory notions.

Because his position is self-contradictory, we should be suspicious of the arguments used to support it. Two arguments bear scrutiny. First, he argues that a person's actions, once done, are now determined, though at the time at which the person performed them, they were free. From this Geisler concludes that "there is no contradiction between an event resulting from a totally free choice and at the same time being completely determined" (pp. 73-74). But this conclusion does not follow, for the action was not determined *at the time* it was performed. It was determined only after it was performed. It was determined in the sense that it cannot be altered once performed.[3] Accordingly, Geisler's appeal to the fact that past free events can no longer be altered is irrelevant to showing that an act can be both determined and free *at the time of its performance*.

In his second argument (p. 70), Geisler contends that since God is simple, all his properties are one with his essence. Thus, the properties of (fore)knowledge and (pre)determination are one in God.[4] That is, they are coextensive. What God determines and what he knows are identical. But from God's simplicity it does not follow that the two have the same content. For example, God's will is also an essential attribute of God. But if Geisler is correct, what God wills would be coextensive

---

[3]Note that *determined* here has a different meaning than used above. Here it means unchangeable or unalterable.

[4]Geisler coins the phrase *knowingly determines and determinately knows* to expound his position. But though this is catchy, what does it mean? That God determines knowingly is ambiguous. It seems to mean that God determines things on the basis of his knowledge, but on his knowledge of what? At one point Geisler suggests that it is on the basis of what he sees persons doing (pp. 73-74). Yet Geisler elsewhere rejects knowledge as the basis for the determination (pp. 70-71, 78). What then does it mean to determine knowingly, if knowledge is not the basis? As for the second, what does it mean to determinately know? It here cannot mean the same thing as in the first phrase, for in the first phrase *determines* refers to God's acts, whereas here it refers to God's knowledge. Does it mean that God's knowledge is definitely settled by what he wills? But then his knowledge is of what he wills or decides, and thus is subjectively, not objectively based. Does it mean that God knows definitely and certainly? But this is a tautology, for with God to know is to know with certainty.

with what he knows and determines. But then, since God knows every-thing we do, he would will our doing evil, which plainly contradicts God's goodness and Geisler's later distinction between divine decree and divine desire.

In sum, not only is his position contradictory, but his arguments which allegedly support it are defective.

Finally, Geisler's position should give Fred some serious second thoughts. For one thing, if it is a sovereign obligation to help others, Fred might well wonder why God himself is not more active in reliev-ing the plight of the poor. After all, according to Geisler, God controls and determines every event. If both Fred's riches and the starving per-son's poverty are from God, it would seem that God himself could right the situation. If God desires good for all and wants all to be saved and if God effectively achieves his purposes, Fred might begin to doubt either God's existence and nature or, more likely, Geisler's particular interpretation of divine sovereignty and human freedom.

Geisler attempts to avoid this unhappy predicament by making a distinction between God's decrees and God's desires. The former is related to God's sovereignty. He decrees everything. The latter is relat-ed to God's goodness. He desires only good. But will this distinction work? For one thing, early in the chapter we were told that God does whatever he pleases, and that no plan of his is thwarted. If a person does what he pleases, he does what he desires to do. And if God desires only good, it should follow from this that only good results. Whence then is evil?

Second, does this distinction make sense? To make a decree is to state that something should be a certain way. Since God's decrees are part of his sovereignty, this should mean that every event not only *should* but *will* occur as decreed. But what would a good God decree to happen? Surely what he decrees must stem both from his desires (otherwise he would act irrationally) and from his moral character (else he would not be good). It is impossible for God to decree something which he does not desire and is inconsistent with his goodness. But if God as good desires what is good, then God can only decree good, not both good and evil. And if this is so, whence is evil and sin, and how could Mary miss God's best for her life?

Geisler tries to avoid this by making a distinction between different kinds of divine wills: prescriptive, permissive and providential. But there is no sense to the first unless humans are free, and it is this which we have found to be impossible on his view. As to the second, how can a God who is sovereign in Geisler's sense allow or permit sin? If God determines and controls everything and his purposes cannot be frustrated, God should not, indeed *cannot*, permit anything of the sort. That leaves us with the third kind of divine will—and with the hard determinism Geisler has tried to avoid.

Fred would be justified in doubting this interpretation of divine sovereignty, a view which attributes both his riches and the poverty and starvation of those in need to God and which at the same time says he should work to alleviate the hunger with his plenty. And Mary should stand incredulous. How could a God who purposes her good determine her to miss God's best? Something has gone amiss, and it is with neither God's sovereignty nor human freedom. I suggest that it is with Geisler's own analysis.

Clark Pinnock's Response

THE GOOD NEWS IS THAT GEISLER, LIKE REICHENBACH AND ME, DEFENDS a strong view of human freedom and a soft view of divine sovereignty. People freely choose what they do, including the all-important decision of whether to accept salvation. God created us with freedom and left its use to us. Geisler is an Arminian.

The bad news is that Geisler tries to combine this view with Thomistic metaphysics, and this places freedom in severe danger. Whereas Reichenbach and I make certain revisions in the theism stemming from Augustine in order to preserve creaturely freedom, Geisler does not, and thus imperils such freedom. Geisler's God eliminates freedom just as surely as Edwards's God does, only in a different way.

How is that? Geisler, following his mentor Thomas Aquinas, puts biblical and Greek ideas together in a synthesis which tends to rule out genuine contingency. One can affirm freedom in this context, but the reality of it will fade away to the degree that the implications of Thomistic theism are realized.

First, in line with Thomistic natural theology, God must be the wholly immutable ground of the contingent and changing world. While this may serve as a good explanation of the existence of the world, it creates a real problem for God's relation to history. If God is immutable, that is, if he cannot change in any way at all, how can he interact with free persons and be affected by them as the Bible says? How can he even contemplate a changing historical scene without running the risk of learning something new? He can do so only if events are not genuinely contingent and thus cannot produce new knowledge. Geisler's theism is at war with his belief about human freedom.

To have freedom you must have genuine alternatives. A person cannot be blamed for stealing if she could not have done anything else. But according to Geisler's theism the whole of history down to the last detail is all fixed and settled in God's mind and cannot be changed in the slightest by anything you or I may decide. Temporal reality is frozen solid. If there were any genuine novelty in it as a result of really free actions, God's immutability would be shattered. Therefore, there must be no novelty, and thus no real freedom. Geisler, like Thomas, wants to have his cake and eat it too. It cannot be done. If God is changeless in every aspect of his being and knows history, there cannot be genuine freedom. If there is real contingency and God knows it, God cannot be changeless in all respects. Geisler's philosophy contradicts itself.

Second, Geisler hopes that the difficult category of timelessness will rescue him from this dilemma. Perhaps if we say God is timeless, we can have both sovereignty and freedom, immutability and change. Alas, nothing is gained by making this move. Bringing Plato's view of time into theology only succeeds in making things worse. On the one hand, how is a timeless God supposed to act the way the biblical God is said to act? A timeless being cannot deliberate or anticipate or remember. It cannot do anything or respond to anything. There cannot be any before or after. In short it cannot be the divine Agent we love and worship. And even worse for Geisler's proposal is the fact that timelessness destroys temporal distinctions and rules out the genuine novelty which results from true freedom. It is a mystery to me why anyone would suppose that timelessness would help him defend human freedom. It would be easier to use timelessness to disprove freedom. Future choices are just as fixed as past choices because they all exist in a timeless present somewhere. You might as well forget about the genuine alternatives which freedom requires. Geisler's solution is a pseudosolution.

Third, despite his attempt to explain it away, Geisler's view of divine
omniscience rules out his view of freedom. If God knows the truth
about the universe down to the last detail, including every choice you
and I will ever make in the future, then we cannot speak of real freedom. The future must be completely determinate and our choices already fixed and certain. Gone is the reality of free choice on our part.
If God knows the future in each detail, then what is going to happen
is fixed and changeless in its entirety. Obviously this has implications
too for theodicy—it spoils the so-called free-will defense on which
Augustine and Thomas depend. Adam could not have done otherwise
than he did given omniscience defined in the strong sense. The fall into
sin was certain before Adam was born.

Fortunately, as I have argued elsewhere in this volume, omniscience
in the sense of a complete knowledge of all future contingents does not
make sense and is not required by the Bible. God knows everything that
can be known, just as he can do whatever can be done. But he does
not know what is unknowable, and cannot do what is undoable. Future
choices made freely are not knowable by any being, for the simple
reason that there is nothing yet to be known. Future decisions are
future—they do not exist in any sense until they are made. Therefore,
it is no deficiency in God's omniscience that he does not know them.
He knows everything that can be known. I discuss the Bible's view of
God's knowledge in my essay and in my response to Reichenbach. The
Bible presents us with a God who faces the future as an open possibility. Some of it is determined by what has already happened, but
much of it is open to God's action and to human freedom. This means
that we can be coparticipants in shaping what will occur.

What Geisler needs, if he is to affirm the view of freedom he defends,
is a more scriptural and dynamic theism. I know that he wants to
identify the Thomistic view with the orthodox view and place others
like me who disagree with him on the edge or maybe outside the limits
of the true faith. But we cannot accept such dogmatism. The fact is
that Geisler's theism is defective biblically and philosophically. The
Greek model of the immutable divinity which he has adopted does not
agree with biblical personalism. The God of the Bible is the loving God
who interacts with his creatures in a changing situation. His experience
of the world is open and not closed. He learns about our decisons as

they happen, not before they happen. While God's character remains the same, his experience of the world is open and he is involved in the ongoing course of events. Philosophically speaking, it is impossible to maintain a static deity ruling over a dynamic universe. When one tries to unite the Greek metaphysic and the Hebraic story of salvation, the two will not stick.

Geisler's advice to Fred and Mary is quite sound because he does not admit to the problem his theism creates for creaturely freedom. He believes in creaturely freedom and advises them on the basis of it. Unfortunately for them, the theistic basis of his advice is filled with difficulties which they would realize as soon as they thought about it. All things happen exactly the way they necessarily must happen so there is no point of any of these anxieties.

III
God Limits His Power

God Limits His Power

Bruce Reichenbach

PUZZLES ARE BOTH MAGNETIC AND ENIGMATIC. SEEING MULTI-shaped pieces strewn across a table leaves us dissatisfied. We cannot pass the random array without feeling the need to place a few in their proper locations, and we end up "hooked," feeling obliged to position "just one more piece."

Puzzles also present enigmas. When we purchase a puzzle, we look not merely for the beauty or artistry of the picture on the box cover, but also for the challenge that it represents. We select puzzles with a large number of pieces, substantial areas of similar shading, or repetitive design. The puzzle presents us with a difficulty which captivates, challenges and at times frustrates. Of course, the pieces all fit together; the trick is achieving that fit.

The problem of this book is like a puzzle. It is both magnetic and enigmatic. Theologians, philosophers and Christians in general have been drawn repeatedly to the question of the relation of God's sovereignty to human freedom. Some have touched on the problem merely in passing; others have treated it in great detail. It has been the source of bitter theological contention, for example between Augustine and the Pelagians and between the Calvinists and Remonstrants. Each thinker lingers over the puzzle, hoping to put that "one more piece" into place. Perhaps you find yourself in such a position, affirming that you will put this book down after just "one more view."

The problem of divine sovereignty and human freedom is enigmatic as well. It appears to be not merely a puzzle with a variety of pieces, but one in which the pieces do not fit together.

In what follows I want to see whether we can construct a coherent, finished picture from the pieces. The puzzle pieces have come to us in a bag without any picture of the finished product. Only the Puzzle-maker knows the finished masterpiece. Thus limited to the disjointed pieces, we begin our attempt to construct a unified whole. To some our construction might seem somewhat strained, as if we have left out some pieces or forced other pieces together. Others might think we have made a good beginning. Each puzzler must decide.

What are the pieces of the puzzle? I think there are six. There are human freedom, God's sovereignty, God's omnipotence, God's omniscience, God's relation to time, and God's involvement in human affairs (providence). In what follows I want to turn the pieces face up, look at each of them to see what they mean, argue for the genuineness of each for the Christian world view, and suggest how they might best be fitted together.

Human Freedom

The first puzzle piece concerns human freedom. To say that a person is free means that, given a certain set of circumstances, the person (to put it in the past tense) could have done otherwise than he did. He was not compelled by causes either internal to himself (genetic structure or irresistible drives) or external (other persons, God) to act as he did. Though certain causal conditions are present and indeed are necessary for persons to choose or act, if they are free these causal conditions are not sufficient to cause them to choose or act. The individual is the sufficient condition for the course of action chosen.

Let me give an illustration. Suppose there is a chocolate-covered filbert on the table in front of me. If I am free, I can either eat the filbert or not eat it, given the causal conditions at the moment. Of course, certain conditions must exist to make my eating it possible: the filbert must be here, it must be edible, I must have a mouth, and so on. But in those cases where I am free, though the filbert is present and I really like filberts, neither the mere presence of the filbert nor my liking of filberts causes me to eat. On the other hand, if there were something in my genetic constitution which made eating filberts a compulsion, such that the mere presence of a filbert was enough to cause me to eat it no matter what my resolution, then I would not be free. Similarly, if there were someone who was stuffing them down my throat or in some other way compelling or coercing me to eat them, I would not be free.

I am not describing or advocating a radical freedom where our choices are made completely independent of causal conditions or where no restraints are placed on us. Freedom is not the absence of influences, either external or internal. Filberts must be present in order for me to eat them. Rather, to be free means that the causal influences do not determine my choice or action. Freedom, as actually found in our experience, is a relative notion: there are degrees of freedom. But where we are free, we could have done other than we did, even though it might have been very difficult to do so (as it is for me to resist filberts).

Second, to view freedom in this way does not mean that our choices are arbitrary or that the acts we perform are the products of chance. There are often reasons which can be given for the actions chosen, reasons of varying soundness and appeal, but reasons nonetheless. These reasons might include the desired ends. For example, to purchase a loaf of bread would be a reason for going to the store. Or the reasons might include a person's likes and dislikes. For instance, I buy an ice cream cone because I like butter pecan ice cream. Liking a certain kind of ice cream did not cause me to buy it, although it was a factor in my buying not only ice cream but a particular flavor. Free persons can accept reasons which are sound and rationally persuasive or they can reject the most telling reasons and choose according to others. Whichever is the case, the action or choice often can be explained. It is not arbitrary simply because it is made freely.

There are two kinds of evidence supporting human freedom. On the one hand, there is universal, introspective evidence. We feel that we have choices—I could have chosen to play racquetball today rather than work on this chapter; I could have selected tomato soup rather than cannelloni from the cafeteria. But choice makes sense only if we can meaningfully select between the options, if we could have chosen or acted differently.

The other kind of evidence is more philosophical. Persons are essentially capable of performing actions which are right or wrong (what are called morally significant actions), actions for which they can be held morally accountable. But if persons are to be held morally accountable for their actions, they must have been able to have acted differently. If persons are to be held accountable for stealing, it must have been possible for them not to steal under those circumstances. Put generally, if being free means we could have acted differently, then to be able to act morally persons must be free. It cannot be the case that they were compelled to act in a certain fashion. Humans cannot be free if an action taken by another person—human or divine—would compel them to think, will, or act in a certain manner.

This approach to moral behavior is borne out in a related field. The law makes distinctions between murder (where the person could have acted differently) and manslaughter (where some critically relevant factors were beyond the person's control, as when a driver cannot avoid hitting a child who suddenly runs out from between parked cars). Or consider the plea of insanity used to excuse persons who commit murder. That they committed the act is not in question. What is in doubt is whether they did so freely or whether their psychological state was such that they could not have done other than they did.

Scripture does not discuss human freedom per se (though it does discuss freedom in relation to other aspects of our lives, for example the law and sin). But it is filled with instances of posed choices which presuppose freedom. From Adam and Eve's option to obey or disobey (Gen 3) to Moses' presentation of a similar option to Israel (for example, Ex 32 and 33) to Joshua's famous final speech concerning service (Josh 24) to Jesus' presentation of the broad and narrow ways (Mt 7:13-14) significant choices are posed. Further, as Christians we believe that we are under certain moral obligations, not the least of which is to love God and to love our neighbors as ourselves. But commands to act properly and the sanctions imposed on improper conduct only make sense if humans have freedom. God places before us his obligations and at the same time has created us free to accept or reject them.

Divine Sovereignty
The second piece to be fitted into our puzzle is divine sovereignty.

Sovereignty invokes the political relationship of governance. It implies that there are at least two classes of individuals, governors and the governed, between which there is an ordered relationship. The governor or sovereign has both authority and power. The authority is either legislative or executive. In his legislative role, the sovereign creates laws by which the governed are ruled. He or she may create the basic laws (for example write the constitution) or may write subsequent laws which support certain prior laws (what might be called secondary or enabling laws). In the executive role, the sovereign implements those laws. The sovereign also has power, with or without limitations. The relation of the sovereign to the fundamental laws and the source of the sovereign's authority help determine the kind of powers the sovereign has, what their limits are, and to what extent they may be employed. If there are certain necessary laws, the sovereign's power is determined and limited by these laws. If the power of the sovereign is derived from the consent of the governed, then his power will be limited by the governed, whose consent may be withdrawn under certain circumstances. Historically, unauthorized taxations and military conscription are examples of such circumstances.[1]

To be sovereign does not mean that everything that occurs accords with the will of the sovereign or that the sovereign can bring about anything he or she wants. The ability of the sovereign to determine the outcome depends, in part, on the freedom granted to the governed. If those subject to the sovereign have freedom, then there are certain things that the sovereign cannot bring about. For example, the sovereign cannot make the subjects freely acknowledge his sovereignty. The sovereign can compel his subjects to bow in his presence, but he cannot compel them to bow freely. And the more freedom the sovereign grants his subjects, the less he can control their behavior without withdrawing the very freedom granted. In granting significant freedom to his subjects, the sovereign makes it possible for his authority and will to be resisted. If the sovereign commands his subjects to do some act and if the subjects are free, they can refuse—though at the same time they

---

[1] It is also the case that *sovereignty* frequently connotes excellence, glory and majesty, but this is not part of its designation. A sovereign could be supremely evil or live in poverty or squalor.

must bear the consequences of their refusal. The sovereign might be able to make them act as he desires, but only at some great cost to other aspects of the sovereign's program. For example, if the sovereign seeks to eliminate certain evils which have resulted from granting freedom of expression (for instance, writing and distributing pornographic material) he might at the same time have to limit in some more general way the dissemination of thoughts and ideas.

Orthodox Christians hold that God is sovereign; he has both authority and power over his creation. We find indicators of this in both the Old Testament (1 Chron 29:11; Ps 115:3) and the New Testament (the parable of the rich householder in Mt 20:1-16 and the analogy of the potter in Rom 9:19-24). The foundation for God's position is not a social contract, but the fact that he is the creator and sustainer of the universe. God has made all things and continues to uphold the universe by "his word of power" (Heb 1:3; see also Neh 9:6; Ps 104:29; Col 1:17). A heightened notion of divine sovereignty is founded on a kind of social contract. God chose to make a covenant with a certain people. Through them all the nations of the earth would be blessed. In this theocratic state all the laws were of divine origin. Thus divine sovereignty was more directly exercised over those who put themselves under the covenant. When the Israelites wanted a mortal king so they would be like the nations around them God expressed dissatisfaction, for he alone was to be Israel's king (1 Sam 8:7-9). The church as the new Israel stands in a similar relationship to God's special sovereignty under the new covenant (Gal 6:15-16; Heb 7:22).

One must be very clear to distinguish the sovereign from the novelist. The novelist creates his own characters, plot, setting, and outcome. All of the participants in the storyline do exactly what the author determines. All have their traits laid out by and have no existence apart from the author. The plot moves inexorably to the end determined by the author. What he desires is precisely what occurs; there can be no variation.

God in his role as sovereign has frequently been confused with the novelist. It is claimed that God has the ability to determine who is created, what they are like, what they will do and say, what the detailed plot is, and how it will all turn out, not just in general but for each individual.

But this is hardly an adequate view of divine sovereignty, for over whom is God sovereign? On this view he is not sovereign over creatures who can freely respond to him. Indeed, there is no real freedom in this scenario. As in the novel, the participants at best have an apparent or illusory freedom. They think that they are free and that their choices are their own. But in fact God has brought it about that they cannot but choose in a given fashion. The creation consequently turns out to be a well-orchestrated novel, deceptive at best in giving an illusion of freedom, rather than a story of divine sovereignty over responsive and responsible creatures.

Omnipotence

The third piece of the puzzle interlocks with the second and concerns another property which orthodox Christians ascribe to God, namely, omnipotence. Literally, *omnipotent* means "all-powerful." It is said that a being who is omnipotent is capable of bringing about anything. However, there are good reasons not to accept this as an adequate definition of omnipotence, for there are some things that it is impossible for this—or any—being to bring about. Yet this inability would not impugn its omnipotence. For example, an omnipotent being cannot create a circle that is square nor cause another person to perform a free act. The former is obvious, for roundness is logically incompatible with squareness. A contradiction is likewise involved in the second case, for an act cannot both be free and caused by another. In short, there are certain things of a self-contradictory or absurd nature which it is impossible for an omnipotent being to do. However, these impossibilities do not tell against its omnipotence, for in fact these things cannot be done by anyone.

Consequently, one might state that a person is omnipotent if he meets two conditions: (1) he can do any action which is not contradictory or absurd; and (2) no being with greater power can be conceived.[2]

Though the Scriptures contain no explicit statement concerning

---

[2]For a more detailed analysis of omnipotence, see my *Evil and a Good God* (New York: Fordham Univ. Press, 1982), chap. 8.

God's omnipotence[3] nor discuss it in a philosophical way, there are some verses which seem to support the claim that God meets the first criterion of omnipotence. For example, "I know that thou canst do all things, and that no purpose of thine can be thwarted" (Job 42:2) and "Whatever the LORD pleases he does, in heaven and on earth, in the seas and all deeps" (Ps 135:6).[4] That the Scriptures affirm the second condition is less clear. God is revealed as claiming that he alone is God and that there is no other god besides him. For example, "See now that I, even I, am he, and there is no god beside me; I kill and I make alive; I wound and I heal; and there is none that can deliver out of my hand" (Deut 32:39).[5] Though this merely affirms that there *is*—and since God is the eternal I Am, always will be—no being with greater power, one can reasonably extend the comparison made with alleged claimants to the title of god to all possible beings. Not only is there no being other than Yahweh who is God, and not only will there never be such a being, but there can be no such being. No possible claimant could ever be God or equal to him. In short, a just concept of the biblical God would be that not only is there no being like him in power, but there can be no such being. God is omnipotent.

Our omnipotence puzzle piece has an important appendage which connects it to the human freedom piece, namely, that it is not inconsistent with God's omnipotence that he limit himself or his activity. In particular, God limits himself in the creation of individuals who are free. God cannot, without destroying our freedom, control us or compel us to choose to act in ways that accord with his will or plan. If God has created us free to choose to love and serve him, then God cannot cause us to do so. It is up to us to accept or reject the grace offered us through the redemptive act of Christ. We are not tools to be ma-

---

[3]The Old Testament *shaddai* should be understood as almighty rather than as omnipotent. Similarly the New Testament *pantokrator* or "ruler of all things" refers "not so much to God's activity in creation as to His supremacy over all things [as over against power over all things]. The description is static rather than dynamic. Hence it has only a loose connection with the dogmatic concept of divine omnipotence, which is usually linked with the omnicausality of God." Gerhard Kittel, ed., *Theological Dictionary of the New Testament*, vol. 3 (Grand Rapids, Mich.: Eerdmans, 1965), p. 915. See also P. T. Geach, "Omnipotence," *Philosophy* 48 (1973): 7-9.

[4]See also Gen 18:14; Ps 115:3; Jer 32:27; and Mt 19:26.

[5]See also Deut 4:35, 39; Is 43:11; 44:8; 45:5-7.

nipulated by God or other persons to achieve their end. Rather, we are conscious beings who should be persuaded to freely live according to God's will and commands.

This is not to say that God (or we, for that matter) should never compel or coerce others to act, that the relations we have with others can never limit, restrict and even deny their freedom. God does at times restrict human freedom. For example, his rescue of Peter from prison restricted the freedom of the jailor. Similarly we restrict the freedom of others; by closing the cellar door I restrict the movement of my two-year-old, Rachel. But when persons must be manipulated or restricted (as, for example, when we must forceably restrain one person from harming another), it must be recognized that such manipulation and interference can destroy the personhood of the individual. Thus, interference which restricts human freedom cannot be condoned without just cause or good reason. And interference which would totally remove morally significant freedom, the freedom to make our own moral choices, is completely dehumanizing and unacceptable. Full humanization and moral growth occur when freedom is encouraged.[6]

Omniscience
The fourth puzzle piece is God's omniscience. To be omniscient is to know all truths. Depending upon God's particular relation to time, this knowledge is either concurrent with all events (if God is atemporal or timeless) or prior to the event (if God is in time, experiencing duration or time-sequencing). In the latter case—which is the sense in which I will treat it—it makes sense to speak of God's foreknowledge, that is, of God's knowing something before it actually happens.

God's omniscience is beautifully portrayed in Psalm 139. The psalmist writes that everything about him is known by God, from his physical being in his mother's womb to his very thoughts even before expressed. He cannot hide from this knowledge—neither direction nor darkness nor death can interfere with it. "Such knowledge," he confesses, "is simply too wonderful for me."

It has sometimes been held that omniscience, interpreted in the sense

---

[6]For a discussion of why self-limitation does not impinge on God's omnipotence, see my *Evil and a Good God*, pp. 165-68.

of foreknowledge, is incompatible with human freedom. It is argued that since God at all times knows all truths, he knows our decisions and actions before they occur. But if God knows what will occur before it happens, what occurs cannot be different from what God knows. Otherwise God would hold a false belief, which is impossible because it contradicts his omniscience. But if we cannot do anything other than God knows, we are not free.

To argue in this way is to confuse the order of causes (what brings something about) with the order of knowledge (the basis on which we know something). What God knows is the event itself. Thus God will know the event if and only if the event occurs. That is, God will have a certain belief about an event occurring if and only if that event occurs. It is because (in a noncausal sense having to do with our knowledge) the event occurs that God believes it occurs. But then one cannot turn around and make the event depend on God's knowledge of the event, as the objector does when he says that God's foreknowledge determines, for the foreknowledge depends upon the event, and not vice versa. For example, God believes that I write this sentence because it is true that I write it. And it is true that I write it because of the fact that I write it. In a trivial sense it is true that if God believes that I will write it, I will write it. But God's knowledge does not cause me to write it. Rather my writing it makes God's belief that I write it true. In short, one must be careful not to confuse the conditions which provide the basis for our knowledge of what happens with the conditions which cause the event to happen. Knowing something to be true does not make the event occur.

We might put this argument another way. The objector contends that no one has the power to act so that the past would be different than it was. Though this is true in a nonrelational sense—one cannot alter facts about the past which have no intrinsic relation to the present—it is not true in a relational sense. For example, I have the power to act so that Martin Luther was born exactly 502 years before I wrote this paragraph by writing it on November 10th, 1985. However, I also have the power to act so that Martin Luther was not born exactly 502 years before I wrote this by delaying my writing. Here I have the power to act so that the past is different than it was, because what is brought about is relationally dependent on the present. Of course, my power is limited. I do not have it in my power to act so that, by writing this now, Martin Luther landed on the moon 502 years before I wrote this. My power relates only to the part having to do with me. But this is what is involved with respect to God's foreknowledge. What God knows about the acts of a person is relationally dependent on what the person who is the object of that knowledge does. Thus, in this relational sense a person has the power to act so that the past is what it is, that is, that God truly believes something about the present. Consequently, there is no contradiction between my human freedom and divine foreknowledge.

Above we distinguished between God as the sovereign creator and God as the novelist. This distinction also has relevance here. It is often held that God foreknows everything that could possibly happen and all individuals who could possibly exist, and on the basis of this knowledge can choose to create a world where everything is harmonious and where his purposes and intents are realized.

Now it is true that the novelist has this kind of knowledge. She knows what each of her characters would do in every situation. But this is because her characters have no freedom; what they "choose" is determined by the author. But God is not the world-novelist. Though he knows all truths, including truths about what free persons choose, he does not know what free persons would choose were conditions different from what they are or about the choices which would be made by possible but never-existing individuals. The reason for this is that statements about what persons would have chosen to do under certain conditions which never came about (what are called counterfactual conditionals of free will) are not true. For example, there is no way of knowing whether I would have eaten at George's if I had driven to Chicago today. Since I did not go there, no one can say what my choice would have been, though one might conjecture what it might have been, based on my character or past choices. But to be part of God's knowledge, counterfactual conditionals of free will must be true. They are not true because they correspond with what actually happens, for as counterfactuals what they describe will never occur—I really did not drive to Chicago or eat at George's. Since these choices will never be made by actually existing individuals, nor with respect to possible people will such individuals ever exist in order to make these choices, they are not simple matters of God's foreknowledge. Neither are they true in that they follow necessarily from certain conditions, for this is inconsistent with their being about possible free choices or actions. Neither are they true in that they correspond with or follow from the person's character or intentions, for a free person can act out of character or change his intentions—I might have decided I was not hungry for a steak and preferred the seafood at The Wharf. In sum, God's knowledge of the characters of his creation is not parallel to that of the novelist, for counterfactual conditionals about free acts of actual or possible persons cannot be true and hence could not be part of God's knowledge.

What this means is that the picture which portrays God as sitting in the heavens, knowing not only what will happen but also how everything would turn out if people chose in other ways or had other people existed, is mistaken. In granting us freedom God has given us the ability to react to different possibilities and knows what will occur. But he does not and cannot know what would have happened if we had acted differently than we did. This means that God does not know what choices you would have made tomorrow if you had done things differently today. This is not because God is limited, but because there is no way of determining what would have happened. Its truth cannot be ascertained.

God and Time

The fifth puzzle piece links with the piece on omniscience and concerns God's relation to time. God cannot be the sort of being who can come into or pass out of existence. He is essentially eternal. But how are we to understand this eternality? The history of Christian theology has understood eternity in two ways. Some have believed that God exists outside of time, never experiencing duration. Others have held that God exists in time, experiencing unending duration; that is, his existence is indefinitely extended both backward and forward in time.

The view that God has no duration (is timeless) entered into Christian theology from Greek thought. It was introduced because some thought that it was most consistent with the fact that God is immutable and perfect. Since change requires that the object which changes be different at two moments of time, a timeless being is incapable of changing. This applies not only to a timeless God's nature (in that none of his essential properties can be altered or lost) but to all his attributes. We might term this *maximal immutability*.

But such a timeless God is the God of Greek philosophy rather than of the Bible. Productive actions are necessarily time-bound and sequential. There is a time prior to the causal event when the person had not acted to produce and there is a subsequent time when he acts to produce the effect. Otherwise one cannot account for the production of the effect at a given time. Consequently, maximal immutability and timelessness are properties incompatible with a being who is productive.[7] The Judeo-Christian God is productive, both in terms of his original creation and his continuous creative activity. At a particular time he brought the universe into existence by his word. He continues to be creatively involved in that world through activity which we term miraculous. In particular, he responds to the petitions of his people, an action which is necessarily sequential since it involves his acting after the petition. And he reveals himself and his will sequentially (Eph 3:1-12). This is most importantly the case when he became incarnate at a particular (that is, at the right) time (Gal 4:4).

Further, a timeless God is incompatible with scriptural descriptions of some of God's mental acts.[8] To consider just one example, Scripture states that God remembers or forgives our sins (Ps 25:7; 79:8; 86:5; Lk 11:4). Or, more theologically, the redemption achieved by Christ alters our position before God, so that while he once considered us sinners, he no longer does (Rom 5:8-9). But remembering and forgiving are acts which are meaningless without the rememberer or forgiver experiencing a before and after.

Someone might, of course, contend that such language contains mere anthropomorphisms or analogies. But if the former, there is little left in revelation to inform us about the character of God himself since most properties which Scripture ascribes to God are time-related. If the

---

[7]Nelson Pike, *God and Timelessness* (New York: Shocken Books, 1970), pp. 104-10.

[8]A God who is timeless is capable of knowing all truths and everything that happens, for the act of knowing is not essentially a time-oriented action. Of course, knowing can be time-located: for example, one can say that I know something now though I did not know it yesterday. But knowing is not *essentially* time-oriented. However, other mental acts which Scripture predicates of God are essentially time-oriented.

latter, then one must show that God and humans do not share the temporal aspect of the analogy. But there is no good reason for making this move, for time predicates which cannot be so easily removed are found in other contexts. For example, God could not have foreknowledge of an event at a time prior to its occurrence (Rom 8:29) nor have chosen us before the foundation of the world (Eph 1:4) if he did not exist in time. But more importantly it seems quite impossible to delete the temporal aspect of God without altering the essential meaning of the terms used to describe him. What, for example, can it mean to say that God remembers, forgives, or reveals unless God as the rememberer or forgiver or revealer experiences sequential duration?

In sum, timelessness is inconsistent with the scriptural God. God sovereignly and providentially intervenes in nature and human affairs, and this intervention is sequential.

What then of God's unchangeableness (immutability)? Must this be denied by someone who believes God experiences duration? Hardly. God is immutable, but his immutability must be properly understood. On the one hand, God is unchanging in his basic nature and character. He was, is, and remains a divine spirit, eternally existent, omniscient, good, merciful, loving and just (Ps 102:27; Jas 1:17). Because he never varies in his character he can be relied upon (Mal 3:6).

On the other hand, God is changing in his consequent nature; that is, in the way these divine properties are manifested in the world. God is in constant, creative relation with his world. He interacts with free individuals whom he has created to have stewardship over that world. Thus, as the world and people change in relation to each other and God, so God changes in relation to them. With respect to his omnipotence, he voluntarily limited his power when he created free creatures. With respect to love, he shows this in various ways at various times, sometimes through pity (Joel 2:18; Ps 103:13; Is 63:9), sometimes through discipline (Ps 118:18; Heb 12:6), sometimes through blessings (Ps 23:5). With respect to his purposes, in essence they remain the same, though in their particulars and in the manner in which God works to realize them he is in constant dialog with those whom he seeks to persuade to help realize his ends on earth. Let me mention just two examples. At various times God repents over the course of action he has chosen because his people fail to follow his guidance and respond to his direction. In such cases God chooses other vehicles to realize his plan (1 Sam 15—16). Or again, God purposes to take certain retributive actions. But when those who sinned repent, he expresses regret over having considered such punishment and forgives those who repented (Ex 32:12, 14; Ps 106:45; Jon 3:10).

In all this, Scripture reveals a God, unchanging in character, dynamically involved in and with his creation, seeking to realize his plans and purposes. He persuades, punishes and rewards, makes covenants and new covenants, all to bring about his ends. But this already links us with the final piece of our puzzle, God's providence. To this we now turn.

Providence

Originally, *providence* meant "to foresee." However, as applied to God, providence refers to his guidance of and care for his creation. Divine providence includes two aspects. On the one hand it involves God's wisdom revealed in his plans and purposes, by which he directs us to that which is good for us. On the other hand it refers to God's power, by which he attempts to realize these purposes by his actions in the cosmos and, more especially, in the affairs of humanity.

To say that God has purposes and plans, however, says nothing about their scope. (Is every detail of human history and experience purposed or part of those plans?) Likewise, it says nothing about the governance or way these purposes and plans will be realized (for example, whether God will directly or indirectly realize them). It says nothing about whether the purposes necessarily will be realized (whether God's purposes can be thwarted). And it says nothing about whether God might alter his plans to take account of certain factors. The response to these issues will put our puzzle together.

Scripture reveals that God has purposes which involve both the universe as a whole and particular individuals. For the cosmos God intends to unite all things in heaven and on earth in Christ (Eph 1:10). For human persons he wills that all be saved (2 Pet 3:9), so that they will conform to Christ's image (Rom 8:29) and that he can show "the immeasurable riches of his grace in kindness toward us" (Eph 2:7). For particular individuals he has special purposes and callings. Jeremiah was chosen as a prophet to deliver the word of the Lord (Jer 1:5-9);

Saul was chosen to be God's messenger to the Gentiles (Acts 9:15-16); Peter was selected to feed Christ's flock (Jn 21:15-17). God also has intentions or purposes for groups of individuals, for nations and for his church. For example, he intends to bring the Gentiles into the family of God to be joint heirs with Israel (Eph 2).

To realize his purposes, God institutes certain plans of action. These might involve particular individuals or, corporately, nations. Through Abraham he intended to make a nation through which all nations would be blessed (Gen 12:1-3). God worked through Pharaoh to release Israel from captivity (Ex 9:16), through Nebuchadnezzar and the Babylonians to punish Judah for abandoning God, and through Cyrus to restore Israel to their land (Is 44:28). God became incarnate to redeem humanity and destroy the works of the devil (1 Jn 3:8).

One might see in these actions both the direct and indirect activity of God. On the one hand, God often works through the natural laws which he has established in his creation. He can and does act at times in ways which supervene natural laws. However, if God were *consistently* to interrupt these natural laws, the world would become a chaos in which human moral action would be impossible. Without regularity and order, we could not rationally plan or calculate what actions to take in order to achieve certain goals. Predictions about the results of our and other's actions would be impossible. Suppose we see some person out in the lake calling for help. Should we act, and if so how should we act? If there were no natural laws or if the laws were very frequently violated by God's direct intervention, we would not know whether to jump in to attempt a rescue. We would not know whether the water would drown the person, whether he would be able to get up and walk on it out of the lake, or whether he would simply float like a cork. How we ought to act depends on how we can act, and how we can act depends on our knowledge. In this case it depends on our knowledge of the natural properties of water and their relation to the human body. But without this type of knowledge our own moral activity becomes impossible. Though this does not mean that God cannot act directly in nature, it does mean that God cannot act in a way which would result in destruction of the natural order and consequently in our own inability to act rationally, prudently and morally. This indicates that God generally acts through nature and its laws to achieve his purposes.

God also involves himself directly and indirectly in human affairs. Just as we, at times, compel others to act in a certain way, limiting their morally significant freedom, so God at times seems to have acted directly, that is, in a manner which limited human freedom. For example, Exodus records that God hardened Pharaoh's heart (9:12), though whether this was a direct action of God or the indirect result of Pharaoh's previous decisions is unclear. Yet it cannot be the case that God always works directly to achieve his purposes. To do so would be to remove human freedom and thereby make it impossible for us to respond to him willingly in love and with the aid of the Spirit to choose to do good. It is through persuasion that his intentions are most often realized, for it is persuasion which is most consistent with human freedom and with the moral and spiritual development it makes possible. God calls, woos, cajoles, remonstrates, inspires and loves. Thus we have the picture in Jesus' parable of the landowner who continually sends messengers and finally his son to persuade the tenants to do his will. Of course, in the end the landowner himself comes and judges the tenants. But the judgment is in respect to their free responses to his messengers.

God is a sovereign, not a novelist. He does not purpose or dispose everything that happens; his purposes are both general and specific, but they do not include every detail of human existence.[9] Not only does he work through his created natural law, but just as importantly he has (in part) entrusted his program to the hands and feet of people. This means, of course, that at times his plans and purposes are thwarted. Before the great flood God expressed exasperation at what humanity had become, and he purposed to begin again, if not entirely, at least

---

[9]The implications of this for the human experience of pain and suffering are significant. Though God allows us to experience pain and suffering, that is, though God does not always intervene to prevent evil, it does not follow that God intends or purposes that we suffer it. With respect to moral evil, this means that though God allows us to commit moral evil and has given us the freedom whereby we can choose good or evil, he does not intend that we misuse our freedom to sin. With respect to natural evil, this means that though God allows us to experience pain and suffering and has created a world governed by natural laws which make such suffering likely, he does not intend that pain and suffering. Though he does intervene to remove natural evils, he cannot intervene to remove all natural evils without at the same time destroying the natural order which is necessary for calculating moral action. For a fuller development of this, see my *Evil and a Good God,* chaps. 4 and 5.

through the line of Noah (Gen 6:5-8). King Saul proved to be disobedient to God's commands, and God purposed to establish a new line through David (1 Sam 15 and 16). Even God's ultimate purpose that all persons will acknowledge him as Lord seems to be unrealized. God is making provision for the separation of the sheep from the goats and for some kind of final or ultimate judgment which involves eternal separation from his presence (Mt 25:31-46; 2 Thess 1:7-9). These and many other passages suggest that God's immediate purposes and plans are not always realized, for he has entrusted them to human hands.[10] Thus God at different times must adopt different plans and stratagems so that his ultimate purpose, the unification of the cosmos under Christ, can be achieved. Though God's plans for implementation are different at different times, in response to the actions of those with whom he has covenanted, there is an eternality about his purposes based on his omniscience (Acts 2:23; Eph 3:8-11). "God is not stumped by men's failure to co-operate. There are things that God can do to bring good out of evil—the paradigm being the incarnation and the cross of Christ. But at every point, we realize that God does not fake the story of human action and human history. He may, in the end, overrule men's deeds, but he does so by forgiveness, redemption and grace."[11]

In sum, God is involved in the world in ways which promote his providential and eschatological purposes. But at the same time he is involved in ways which use natural laws and are consistent with, indeed employ, the freedom with which he endowed us.

The Puzzle Completed

The picture should now be whole. God is sovereign in authority and power. Yet at the same time he willingly limited his power and created

---

[10]One can find Paul struggling with this issue in Romans 9. On the one hand, he sees that Israel has not remained true to their covenant, thwarting God's plan of salvation through them. On the other hand, he does not want to see this as a failure of God's word. Thus, he makes the covenant relation dependent on spiritual rather than physical descendency. Not all who are descended from Israel belong to Israel. This leads to his second point, that the implementation of his purposes is done through his selection of his servants, not on the basis of their merit but solely on the basis of his choice.

[11]Brian Hebblethwaite, "Some Reflections on Predestination, Providence and Divine Foreknowledge," *Religious Studies* 15, no. 4 (December 1979): 437.

us with the freedom to choose between good and evil, between God and ourselves. A world in which we are free is necessary if there is to be both moral action and meaningful response to God's overtures of love. Through us he now seeks to realize his intentions and purposes. Of course God is not limited to such methods; he can and does act directly in his creation. The Christian might well contend that were not God directly active in the creation, the world would be a much worse place to live than it presently is. But since many of God's more important purposes have to do with our moral and spiritual development and restitution, God works through natural laws and us to achieve his intentions. God's sovereignty does not necessitate that every human or nonhuman action is predetermined, a part of his plan, or even desired. The sovereign cannot command free obedience. Thus it is that God has taken both indirect and direct action (sending his Son) to call people to repentance, to become his servants in bringing about his kingdom.

To be able to act meaningfully, God must exist in time. Because God is in time, he can act in time and creatively and persuasively work to realize his ends. And most significant of all, he can act in the fullness of time to reconcile human persons who, because of their willfulness, have sinned and alienated themselves both from each other and from God. But despite the human record of broken covenants, disobedience to God and self-seeking, we can be assured that God in his omniscience knows our predicament and continues to be active in human affairs. He continues to respond to human petitions, to purvey his grace, and finally to seek to draw all to himself.

Before we turn to the case studies, a note of caution should be posted. The attempt to apply theological and philosophical reasoning to concrete cases is fraught with danger. For one thing, the practical consequences of a theory depend on the specific facts of the individual case, and it is often difficult to ascertain all the relevant facts in each case. What has been Fred's relations with others in obtaining his wealth? What is Mary's true intellectual potential? For another, God's specific intent for any person is known only to God, unless he reveals it. One can, of course, speak about God's general intent—that all come to know and love him. But the intent he has for specific persons is less clear. This, in a sense, is the point of the second case study. How does one decipher that intent or ascertain God's will? Whatever might be the answer, expectations of definitive answers will probably be disappointed. Only to Mary can God give that personal assurance which will dispel her doubt that in the place where her journey has taken her she is ministering to his kingdom. In this day of modern travel, we expect life to be like a trip where God has already constructed, paved and lined the road, posted all the signs in their appropriate colors, and like the AAA marked out the best route to our final destination. Alas, the human journey is a pilgrimage. The road, though intersecting numerous other paths, has neither been laid nor traveled before, the markers are vague pieces of the landscape, and both the journey and final destination are unclear in their particulars. What we need is not a definitive map, but the confidence that through it all God is our constant companion, "at work in [us], both to will and to work for his good pleasure" (Phil 2:13).

Fred and Fortune

Fred ought both to thank God for the material blessings he has received and to attribute his wealth to the fact that he has been born in a prosperous Western nation and has worked diligently. These are not incompatible. For one thing, the material blessings he has are a result of the general good with which God has blessed his creation. God's created world, by virtue of its very order and nature, makes it possible for Fred to experience good. And by allowing Fred to exist, to freely choose, to think and act and appreciate, God has made it possible for Fred (and others) to prosper. Thus, in this very general sense Fred has much to be thankful for. On the other hand, whether God is more directly involved in Fred's prosperity is difficult to determine. It is possible that for his purposes God has used indirect or secondary causes to bring prosperity to Fred, just as we use the laws of nature to do good to one another. It is a scriptural teaching that God does bless those who love him and seek his will. However, Fred must avoid the error of claiming that his material prosperity is a definite sign or indication of God's blessing. The sun shines and the rain falls on the just and the unjust (Mt 5:45). Since God's blessing is an act of grace and not dependent on merit, there is no necessary connection between material wealth and being in favor with God.

There are several aspects to this. First, to be a child of God is not a bed of roses, materially, psychologically or spiritually. A study of the "giants" of the Bible makes this evident. Joseph spent time in empty wells and dark prisons as well as in palace halls. Moses, who suffered the anguish of leading a nation rebellious both to himself and God, never entered the Promised Land. David endured physical danger, life as a fugitive and his son's treason. Paul's list of sufferings includes dangers from rivers, robbers, countrymen and seas, cold and hunger (2 Cor 11:24-27). Our journey is no less through the valley of death's shadow than over the mountaintop; it is no less one of poverty and privation than of wealth and plenty. God's favor is not to be equated with easy times and material prosperity.

Correspondingly, poverty is not to be equated with God's disfavor. God does not will that people suffer either pain or any form of degradation. Yet at the same time humans do suffer. In some cases it is a punishment from God for their actions; God does discipline his creatures. Yet in this judicial capacity God does not will their suffering, just as he did not will their sin. Yet were God not to punish wrongdoing, his very character would be in question. More often, however, human suffering and degradation are due to the evils which persons inflict on each other. The causes of the ills which humanity brings on itself are complex. Just to consider an example that Fred might ponder, there are numerous factors which result in starvation and malnutrition: overpopulation, warfare, corruption (in the food distribution system and governments), laziness, exploitation, waste, unwillingness to share, and other moral evils. It is frequently humans who bring these evils on themselves or others or who through their action or inaction are morally culpable for not attempting to resolve them.

Fred could rightly ask why God allows this. The response is that God deems it more valuable for there to be free persons who can do good and respond to him in love than for there to be no morally good (or bad) actions and no love responses. As we have seen, moral action requires that persons be free. But granting us freedom not only makes it possible for us to do good and respond to God and others in love, it also allows us to do evil and respond in greedy, selfish and exploitive fashion to one another.

How then is God involved in this world situation? At times directly. There are times when God acts directly to alter the course of nature in order to benefit human beings or achieve his purposes. However, as we suggested earlier, this cannot be the normal manner of divine action, lest it remove the morally significant freedom with which God has endowed us. More often he acts indirectly through the hands and feet of his servants, who respond in specific ways to the needs of others. Thus Fred should thank God for the opportunities and prosperity he has experienced. But he is likewise under obligation to use what he has to minister effectively to those who, for one reason or another, are not so fortunate.

But, Fred might ponder, could not God providentially at least eliminate the worst evils? He gave manna to the Israelites, why not to the starving Somalis? There are a number of responses to this, but for lack of space let me simply note two. The first reason we have already developed. If God did choose to intervene regularly in the natural order to remove suffering, the world would cease to be a theater of moral action. We could not propose goals to be achieved nor calculate how to act to achieve those goals. Granted that God does intervene; his intervention is generally consistent with allowing humans to rationally determine their action and to act in such ways as to respond morally and spiritually to God and others. Second, we should note the principle which underlies this query: God, as good, should intervene to eliminate the worst evils in the world. But "worst evils" is a comparative notion. Suppose that God removed all evils of the magnitude of 10^7. There would still be instances of "the worst evils" in our world, namely, evils of the magnitude of 10^6. The same reasoning would now apply to these evils, requiring that God eliminate these as well. But then evils of 10^5 would be "the worst evils," and the principle would have to again be applied. In short, by consistently applying the principle that a good God is under obligation to intervene to remove the worst evils, we derive the consequence that God is required to remove all evils. But this would require the removal of human freedom and consequently make moral action and the attainment of moral good impossible. But we have noted that God deems these things intrinsically valuable. God has chosen to work through the persons whom he has created, inspiring, persuading, encouraging and commanding them to do his work on earth. And he has chosen this because this is the only way in which moral and spiritual virtues can be realized.

Mary and Monday Morning

There is, in each of us, a Monday-morning quarterback. If something goes well, we wonder whether something we could have done would have made it even better. If something goes poorly, we likewise wonder, "What if. . . ." On the one hand, what-ifs are important questions, for through them we analyze more carefully the causes for what happened. It is a truism that those who fail to pay attention to the past are doomed to repeat its mistakes. So it is important for Mary to reflect on the various causal conditions which led to her medical school rejection. From them she can learn about how to be an effective student or how to carefully choose persons to write recommendations for her or where her true abilities lie.

But on the other hand, there is a tyranny in the what-if. Short of interviewing the selection committee, it is unlikely she will ever know why she was rejected. And even if she did, the tyrannical what-if remains unanswerable, for neither she nor God will ever know the counterfactual conditonals about what would have happened if . . . There is a connection, but not a *necessary* connection between studying hard or having good recommendations and being admitted into medical school.

So where does God fit into this picture? It makes sense, I think, to say that God opens and shuts doors in guiding us to that which will fulfill ourselves and serve his kingdom. God can do this directly, as he did with Paul (though even here he worked through other persons). Or he can do it indirectly through the abilities with which he has endowed us, the opportunities which are made available to or denied us by others, or the natural events we experience and persons we encounter. Of course, we can accept or reject that guidance at any point along the pilgrimage. And should we go in a different direction, God's guidance will adjust itself accordingly (as with both Balaam and Jonah).

It would be devastating for Mary to spend the rest of her life looking back to an event, wondering about "God's best." Through a combination of her own actions, the actions of others, and the circumstances in which she has found herself, she has passed through one of a set of possible doors. She cannot go back; she is now in a new place. New opportunities to develop her own potential and to minister to the needs of others are open to her. It is true that she might have missed opportunities which would have led to her own growth and which might have significantly influenced and affected others. But she cannot dwell on what lies behind the other doors. What remains is for her now to seize the opportunities which God directly and indirectly places before her and in doing so be open to God's guidance in her life.

Human Tapestry

The Lord's Prayer contains the poignant words: "Thy will be done." And so we pray. It seems clear that God's will is not always or even often done, for in turning our backs on God and our neighbor, in refusing to love in the way modeled by Christ, in failing to live out the fruits of the Spirit we reject what God intends for us to do. Thus the words of the prayer call us to alter our lifestyle so that what we do, think, will and say accords with God's expectations of his children. On the other hand, God is sovereign. He is in authority commanding respect and obedience and in power implementing his purposes through his eternal wisdom in ways consistent with the creation of free persons operating in a natural order. God's finale is an intricately woven tapestry produced by billions of hands. God knows the individual weavers—their abilities, shortcomings and in the end the little variegated, irregular patch they will sew. Out of a myriad of pieces he is creating a whole tapestry. Stained with every human imperfection and vice, beautified with every human perfection and virtue, the masterpiece slowly takes shape under his guiding hand, until that day when he has finished it, presenting it splendidly in his new heaven and new earth.

John Feinberg's Response

BRUCE REICHENBACH PRESENTS AN ANALYSIS OF DIVINE SOVEREIGNTY and human freedom from an indeterministic perspective. Since much of what he says does not differ substantially from the views of Pinnock, I shall concentrate on a limited set of items.

As in the case of Pinnock, I have problems with Reichenbach's concept of freedom as it relates to God's control. Reichenbach claims that God can accomplish his ultimate purposes (p. 119), but I wonder how God can guarantee that his ends will be done in virtue of contra-causal freedom. Given such freedom, it must always be possible for someone to overturn God's plans by choosing to do otherwise than God wants.

Another concern is Reichenbach's claim that God limited his power in order to give us freedom (contra-causal, of course). However, as with Pinnock, I wait in vain for a verse that says God did such a thing. Of course, Reichenbach thinks he has proved it by pointing to verses that teach human freedom. But, that only constitutes proof if one assumes that Reichenbach's notion of freedom is the only kind of freedom there is, and of course, that begs the question.

My last claim above raises another problem I have with Reichenbach. He begs the question on the meaning of freedom. In defining freedom, Reichenbach writes (p. 103), "Rather, to be free means that the causal influences do not determine my choice or action." In explaining his notion of omnipotence (p. 107), he claims that God cannot do anything contradictory, and he then explains that *causing* another person to perform a free act is a contradiction, for "an act cannot both be free and caused by another." Other examples could be produced, but these will suffice. Reichenbach's claims are unquestionably true if and only if contra-causal freedom is the only possible kind of freedom. However, Reichenbach's claims about freedom and determinism being contradictory show that he refuses to allow the possibility that a determinist could legitimately talk about freedom. As I have shown, a soft deterministic form of freedom is not an impossibility. Thus, Reichenbach begs the question.

The preceding suggests a related point. Reichenbach seems to think that either one is free (of course, as he defines freedom) or one is causally determined (not free, according to Reichenbach). However, as I read his section on human freedom, I find much with which I can agree. The reason is that his argumentation *for* his form of freedom basically argues *against* a *hard* form of determinism according to which all human actions are coerced and compelled. As it turns out, determinists of this stripe usually admit that their view makes no room for freedom. Since such a view is not the position I hold, I agree with Reichenbach in rejecting hard determinism. However, my problem is that nothing he says in the whole essay offers proof against a soft deterministic notion of freedom (really, Reichenbach doesn't even consider the view) but only against a hard-line determinism.

Another matter of concern is how on a contra-causal notion of freedom one comes to choose. Reichenbach gives more of an explanation on this matter than does Pinnock, but I find it problematic. In explaining that a person does not choose without reason, Reichenbach explains that "free persons can accept reasons which are sound and rationally persuasive or they can reject the most telling reasons and choose according to others" (p. 103). On page 119, Reichenbach explains that by persuading people to act as he wishes God can accomplish his purposes in a way that leaves people free. This is basically what I would say. What is problematic is that Reichenbach does not seem to think such actions are determined. But, by his own explanation, it appears that the reasons he alludes to are part of the causal explanation that even he would give as to why one action was done rather than another. If this is not actually determinism, then we need an explanation as to how it differs. Reichenbach would probably respond that it is not, for reasons are not causes. That is surely a moot matter, and not one we are likely to resolve here. However, my point is that on his own account it appears that such reasons decisively incline the will toward one action rather than another. And, if that is so, it seems rather clear that the action is determined. If Reichenbach responds that such reasons do not decisively incline the will, then I must ask for an explanation of how a person comes to choose! If the answer is that the person just chooses, I want to know how, and I want the answer to be one which does not entail determinism. I see no such answer in Reichenbach.

A final point of some significance is Reichenbach's handling of divine foreknowledge. Reichenbach argues that God does have foreknowledge of future events. He offers an explanation of how foreknowledge fits with his notion of freedom, but I do not see that it works. Much of Reichenbach's discussion (pp. 111-12) focuses on denying that God has middle knowledge, but of course that only shows us how Reichenbach will not try to solve the problem. Reichenbach's explanation actually appears on pages 109-11.

Reichenbach heavily emphasizes the distinction between the order of causes and the order of knowledge. As he notes, God's knowledge of an event does not *cause* it to occur. God cannot know an event if it does not occur, but that does not mean that such knowledge of its occurrence causes it to occur. Thus, "one must be careful not to confuse the conditions which provide the basis for our knowledge of what happens with the conditions which cause the event to happen. Knowing something to be true does not make the event occur" (p. 110).

The above distinction is the heart of Reichenbach's explanation on freedom and foreknowledge, and it is an important distinction. But, will it work? I think not. The initial problem with the explanation is that it misses the point. Reichenbach is surely right that anyone's knowledge (God's included) of what will occur does not make anything occur, but the Calvinist/determinist agrees with that point. The Calvinist/determinist's point is to ask how God can really know (in the strong epistemological sense) that something will occur if in fact it is not set. Obviously, it is not set or caused by anyone's knowledge of it, but the fact that one has knowledge of it suggests that it will in fact occur. Herein lies the problem for contra-causal freedom, for God cannot guarantee that something will assuredly occur if contra-causal freedom is correct. And, if he cannot guarantee it, then at best he thinks it will occur but does not *know* that it will. Thus, Reichenbach's distinction is extremely important in general but irrelevant to the particular issue at hand.

A closer look at Reichenbach's view shows it to be even more problematic. Reichenbach repeatedly states (pp. 110-11) that what makes God's *belief* true is that the event occurs. "What God knows is the event itself. Thus God will know the event if and only if the event occurs. That is, God will have a certain belief about an event occurring if and only if that event occurs" (p. 110). This is truly problematic. If God only believes that something will occur and does not *know* that it occurs until it occurs, then this is tantamount to saying that God does not have *fore*knowledge of the *future* event.

In fairness to Reichenbach, he does not use such temporal language as *when* and *until*, though it would seem that such is his meaning. One could interpret his claims atemporally, but my contention is that whether one interprets his claims temporally or atemporally, Reichenbach has a problem. He claims that God knows the event *if* it occurs. Suppose we interpret this temporally. Then, it must mean that *before* it occurs, God *believes* but does not *know* it will occur. This makes sense, but it denies that God has foreknowledge of future events. On the other hand, let us interpret the claim atemporally. Such an interpretation would seem to entail that God really does *know* the future (forget for the moment discussions of when God knows it). However, if this is what Reichenbach means, then I have to ask how God can *know* the future, given the contra-causal freedom that Reichenbach holds. He may have an explanation as to how God can *know* the future if contra-causal freedom is correct, but surely none appears in his essay.

In sum, Reichenbach's views face the following dilemma: either we interpret his statements temporally and God does not know the future until it occurs (which means he does not know it while it is still future), or we interpret his claims atemporally and God really does have foreknowledge of the *future*, but then Reichenbach's contra-causal freedom is in trouble.

Because of considerations such as these I must conclude that despite his claim that he holds to divine foreknowledge of future events, his discussion does not explain satisfactorily how he leaves a place for such a notion on his account of freedom. My overall assessment of Reichenbach's article is that while it is one of the more carefully argued pieces that one will find from an Arminian/indeterminist position, I am still not convinced by the case he builds.

Norman Geisler's Response

MY BASIC AREA OF AGREEMENT WITH FEINBERG IS WITH HIS VIEW OF GOD.
With Reichenbach, it is with his view of freedom. We both agree: (1)
that free choice implies we could have actually done otherwise; (2) that
free choice has no internal or external compulsion; (3) that there are
influences on free acts; (4) that the human agent himself is the cause
of the free act; (5) that no free act is random or fortuitous. This is what
I called a self-determined (caused by another) or an indetermined (uncaused) act.

My main areas of difference with Reichenbach's views are on the
nature of God. First, for reasons stated earlier, I differ with his view
that sovereignty "does not mean that everything that occurs accords
with the will of the sovereign" (p. 105).

Second, although I agree that God "cannot compel them to bow
freely," I disagree that "the more freedom the sovereign grants his
subjects, the less he can control their behavior" (p. 105). A sovereign,
omniscient God can determine things just as well through his knowledge of free choices as in any other way. He cannot be wrong about
what he knows, even if he knows it will occur freely.

Third, I deny Reichenbach's view that God does not have as much
control over his free subjects as a novelist has over his characters. From
God's eternal standpoint, history is just as determined as the story in

a novel. Yet the moral actions in history were all free. An omniscient God sees "forward" with the same certainty that he sees "backward." Thus to an omniscient mind who knows all of history in a timeless "now" all free events are also determined. To use Reichenbach's illustration, Luther's birthday will never change no matter how far we are removed from it. It is fixed forever, even though his parents exercised some free choice concerning it.

Fourth, Reichenbach weakens considerably the traditional evangelical view of omnipotence when he reduces it to one in which "no being [has] greater power" (p. 107). This would not give God the greatest possible power but only the greatest actual power. Reichenbach thinks God's omnipotence means that "there is no being like him in power, . . . there can be no such being" (p. 108). But this may mean that God can have no equals, not that his power can have no limits. If so, this is not the historical understanding of omnipotence, either Calvinistic or Arminian.

Reichenbach offers no good reason why we should give up the strong sense of omnipotence which is at the heart of orthodox theology. And even though it is currently in vogue to reject the classical orthodox view of God, most have not fully faced the disastrous consequences this will have on the whole of Christian theology.

Fifth, Reichenbach redefines the traditional view of God's omniscience. Rather than God knowing everything that is, as well as what will be, he concludes that "God will know the event if and only if the event occurs" (p. 110). But such a God is severely limited in his knowledge. He is limited by contingent events because he is dependent on their occurring before he can acquire the truth on that subject. But such a limitation does not square with the assertion that God is unlimited in knowledge, which is implied in God's omniscience.

Sixth, I take exception with Reichenbach's claim that either a free act is caused by God's knowledge or else God's knowledge is caused by the free act (p. 110). This is a false disjunction. There is a third alternative: God's eternal knowledge can determine that the act be caused freely. In this case God neither produces the act, nor does the act produce God's knowledge. God simply knows (eternally and determinately) what we choose to do. Thus the act can be both determined from the standpoint of God's knowledge and yet free from the point of view of the agent's choice.

Seventh, I also disagree with Reichenbach's contention that God's knowledge can be changed in the same way we can change truths about the past (relationally). This conclusion is based on his mistaken notion that "what God knows . . . is relationally dependent on what the person . . . does" (p. 111). But an independent Being who is the cause of everything which exists, or ever will exist, is not dependent on his creatures for anything. They are dependent on him. As even Reichenbach admits, all that is necessary for the event to be determined is for God to have infallible (fore)knowledge that it will occur. One would have to prove that God could not have infallible foreknowledge of free acts. But this has not been done. And as long as it is possible for an omniscient God to know future free acts, then it is impossible to prove that he cannot determine the future. And it makes no difference whether God can know what could be as long as he knows what will be. If he knows what will be, then it must be, since an omniscient God cannot be wrong about what he knows will freely happen.

Eighth, I disagree with the implication that the classical theistic view of a timeless God is wrong because it is "from Greek thought" (p. 112). The teaching of an eternal Creator of the temporal world (Gen 1), the I AM of Moses (Ex 3) came long before Greek philosophers. Besides, logic was also developed by the Greeks. But I am sure Reichenbach is not willing to throw out logic because it has a Greek source. To reject something simply because of its source is a genetic fallacy. Yet no argument has been offered which proves that God's essence is time-bound. At best all Reichenbach and others have shown is that "productive actions are necessarily time-bound and sequential" (p. 113). They have not shown that the producing actor must thereby also be time-bound.

Reichenbach also seems to (wrongly) imply that God creates at different times (to God). But if God is eternal then he did not create at different times (to him). God acts in time but he acts from eternity. Hence, the God who creates time cannot be time-bound. If the Creator must partake of the nature of his creation, then God would have to be a creature because he created. Or he would need to have a beginning because the world he made had a beginning.

Ninth, as to what elements in biblical anthropomorphisms and analogies apply to God's unlimited essence and what do not, I would suggest the following: whatever God created which necessarily implies limitation cannot apply to an unlimited God, but whatever perfections he produced which do not imply limits do apply to him. So even though God creates changing, finite things, he cannot actually change in any way or have limited things like arms, ears and eyes. But God is good, true, holy, just, intelligent and powerful, because these are perfections which do not necessarily imply limitations. Thus, while God is one in essence, yet many names (attributes) are true about him. Just as all the radii are one at the center of the circle, so God's many different attributes refer to his absolutely one essence. For no one thing which can be said of God exhausts the profundity of his infinite nature. So while all God's names are said of him, truly they are predicated of him only analogically.[1] In this way God can be absolutely one and yet have many names. Unless an actual contradiction between the definition of one attribute and the definition of another can be demonstrated (which has not been done), there is no inconsistency in affirming more than one thing analogically of the absolutely simple essence of God.

Tenth, I disagree with Reichenbach's assertion that since "people change in relation to each other and God, so God changes in relation to them" (p. 114). This is the fallacy of illicit conversion. Just because all horses have four legs does not mean all four-legged creatures are horses! When a person changes in relation to the pillar, the pillar does not change. Likewise, when we change in relation to God, God does not change.

Finally, an absolutely simple God cannot be "unchanging in character" (p. 115) and yet changing in essence. God's character is one with his essence. But Reichenbach implies that God is not absolutely one but has two opposing natures, a "primordial nature" which is changeless and nontemporal, and a "consequent nature" which is changing and temporal (p. 114). But this is not a historic Christian position at all but a neoclassical, process view of God. A God who can change in his essence is not really God at all; he is a contingent, composed being who needs a Creator. He is merely a being who can come to be rather than

---

[1]See our discussion of analogy in *Philosophy of Religion* (Grand Rapids, Mich.: Zondervan, 1974), chap. 12.

the one WHO IS, the great "I AM." A God who is in the process of becoming is not the God of Abraham, Isaac and Jacob, nor the God of Augustine, Anselm, Aquinas, Calvin or Luther. In fact, such a God is not the Christian God who made us in his image; he is a non-Christian concept of God whom we made in our image.

Clark Pinnock's Response

THIS IS CERTAINLY THE BEST OF THE OTHER ESSAYS FROM MY POINT OF view, and I applaud it. The author is on the right track and has produced a model which is very nearly right. He recognizes significant human freedom, defines sovereignty and omnipotence in a consistent, biblical manner, and presents a sensible view of God's eternity and providential rule. But at one point his logic fails him.

That point is our understanding of the omniscience of God. Reichenbach continues to think of it in classical terms, as involving an exhaustive knowledge of all future contingents, and this simply will not work. To use his image of the puzzle, five pieces belong and fit together nicely, but the fourth piece, omniscience, taken in the way he understands it, is awkward and ill-fitting. The essay is generally coherent, but not at this point. My suggestion, that we rethink what divine omniscience means, would make his model work.

All three of the other essayists agree against me in attributing to God an exhaustive knowledge of all future events, including those which result from the choices of free persons. Feinberg and I see what this implies, but Reichenbach and Geisler do not. If God sees the whole of the future, then the future is fixed and frozen, and we are mistaken to believe that we have the liberty to choose one way or the other. God knows what Reichenbach will do with his piece of candy. So the future is not, as he thinks, a realm of open possibility in which he can by his freedom determine what is true. It cannot turn out different in any respect from what God from eternity has infallibly known it to be. Reichenbach can only choose to do actions which God has always known he would do. Therefore he cannot do otherwise than what he is destined to do. By admitting his view of omniscience, the author has spoiled an otherwise promising model of divine sovereignty and human freedom.

To me this is perfectly clear both philosophically and theologically. In terms of logic it is obvious that a future free decision, defined the way Reichenbach and I both define it, cannot be known ahead of time by God or anyone else. Being a decision that has yet to be made there is nothing for him to know. Future free decisions do not exist anywhere to be picked up on even by an omniscient being. The whole idea of a free action is that the future is open to be determined by that choice when it is made. If the future is exhaustively known, it is not open in the required sense, and freedom is illusory. By taking the view he does, Reichenbach ends up with a future which is fixed and changeless in every respect, and this ruins his whole case.

Theologically speaking, I agree with the Calvinists on this. What God foreknows is as fixed and certain as what God foreordains. The one is as opposed to genuine contingency and freedom as the other. Foreordination renders events certain, but foreknowledge presupposes that they are certain. What God foreknows cannot possibly turn out differently, yet freedom implies that it can. I agree with the strict Calvinists that Arminians, if they wish to be consistent, must rethink the traditional doctrine of omniscience as well as omnipotence. This is what Reichenbach refuses to do.

But the solution is not far away. In respect to omnipotence the author notes that it does not mean the power to do impossible things like squaring a circle. Well then, it is the same in respect to omniscience. Omniscience cannot mean a knowledge of things which cannot be known. God knows everything that can be known, but future free decisions are not there to be known even by God. So his not knowing them in advance is no imperfection in his omniscience. Not knowing them is simply a state of affairs brought on by God's decision to create a world with an open future. I would urge Reichenbach and other

Arminians to be intellectually more courageous and take their position in this direction.

Unfortunately, some will not do so because the traditional way of reading the Bible on divine omniscience is so strong. You see that in Reichenbach's own essay. He thinks that Psalm 139 settles the matter and forces one into the uncomfortable position he has adopted. Even though the reader may give me high marks for clarity, he may well reject clarity in favor of what he conceives to be biblical faithfulness. And I admire that.

But let the reader consider what may seem a faintly heretical possibility. I would contend that the Bible does not represent God in possession of exhaustive knowledge of all future contingents. On the contrary, it presents God as a dynamic agent who deals with the future as an open question. You see that very clearly in the book of Jonah. God had intended to destroy Ninevah, but then something unexpected happened—Ninevah repented. Neither God nor Jonah knew this was going to happen. God approved and the prophet disapproved. As a result God changed his mind and decided not to go through with his plan to destroy the city. You find the same pattern all through the Bible. God plans to punish Israel but Moses intercedes for them and God relents (Ex 32). He tells Jeremiah, if the people repent one thing will follow, but if they do not another thing will happen. Now I ask you, what sense does it make to suppose that God knew all the time the outcomes of events in these situations? It makes no sense at all. In fact it spoils the whole point of the narrative and the reality of the history. I think that the traditional view of omniscience is philosophically untenable and biblically untrue.

But what about predictive prophecy, you say? Well, if you look carefully at it, you will discover that most of it is easily accounted for by God's predicting—on the basis of what he knows—what is going to happen, or by God's announcing ahead of time what he plans to do in such and such a circumstance or by some combination of these two factors. Prophecy is after all profoundly conditional and oriented to our response to God. We are not locked into a future course of events in which what we decide to do has no part to play in how things turn out.

In dealing with the cases of Fred and Mary, Reichenbach does a pretty good job since his model is, as I have said, very nearly perfect. His only problem stems from the inconsistency I have been discussing. If Fred and Mary discover that Reichenbach's view on divine omniscience implies a greater fixity of future events than he wants to admit, they would rightly be troubled and forced to think seriously about it. So let us hope Fred and Mary do not read my essay in this volume.

IV
God Limits His Knowledge

God Limits His Knowledge
Clark Pinnock

T HE BIBLE SEEMS TO BE PRETHEORETICAL IN ITS APPROACH TO the relationship between divine sovereignty and human free-dom. Some passages can be read to support God's determin-ing all things. Others, with equal strength, stress the significant free-dom of human beings. A tension is allowed to stand in the biblical text; a definitive resolution is nowhere attempted.

Ought we even to attempt a resolution? Some theologians have con-cluded we should not. The relation between sovereignty and freedom is an impenetrable mystery transcending human logic, they say, and therefore one should suppress the imperious demands of reason and submit to the antinomy. In an appeal to conservative evangelicals, J. I. Packer concludes that because the Bible teaches both these truths un-mistakably the believer ought to accept them both on the basis of the authority of the Bible.[1]

Unfortunately, that is easier said than done. At several levels the need to try to relate sovereignty and freedom coherently surfaces and will not be suppressed. On one level, thinking Christians who are unaccus-tomed to accepting contradictions in the Bible generally will ask wheth-

---

[1] J. I. Packer, *Evangelism and the Sovereignty of God* (Downers Grove, Ill.: InterVarsity Press, 1961), chap. 2.

er they should accept this contradiction at face value as they are urged to do. They will wonder if the terms have been properly defined, or whether all the possible ways to relate them have been explored.

On a second level, skeptics will ask whether Christian theism is coherent when it affirms sovereignty and freedom at the same time. They will not be impressed if they are told it is an antinomy. Apologists for the faith will want to ask if it is necessary to sacrifice the credibility of the gospel at this point. In the minds of certain atheists belief in divine sovereignty rules out human freedom and makes it impossible to account for evil in the world. The price in terms of evangelism will be high if we can offer no rational hypothesis to explain sovereignty and freedom.

On a third level, we find the practical issues on which this volume is focused. Believers want to know why God planned for tragedy to strike them and why the world has so much misery in it. They will ask, what freedom do I have if God knows every single thing I will ever decide to do? The itch to understand better the relation between divine sovereignty and human freedom will not go away.

But do not despair. There is a way to understand the relationship which satisfies both scriptural data and the requirements of intelligence, a model which does not have to posit a basic contradiction between sovereignty and freedom. Let me summarize it now and then proceed to expound on it.[2]

As Creator of the world God is sovereign in the fundamental sense. He has chosen to bring into existence a world with significantly free agents. In keeping with this decision, God rules over the world in a way that sustains and does not negate its character and structures. Since freedom has been created, reality is open, not closed. God's relationship to the world is dynamic, not static. Although this will require us to rethink aspects of conventional or classical theism, it will help us relate sovereignty and freedom more coherently in theory and more satisfactorily in practice.

---

[2]Another theologian who holds the view I am defending and gives a longer account of it is Richard Rice, *The Openness of God: The Relationship of Divine Foreknowledge and Human Free Will* (Minneapolis: Bethany House Pub., 1985).

The Sovereignty of God

God is sovereign according to the Bible in the sense of having the power to exist in himself and the power to call forth the universe out of nothing by his Word. But God's sovereignty does not have to mean what some theists and atheists claim, namely, the power to determine each detail in the history of the world. Antony Flew is wrong when he says that any sovereign creator must control every thought and action in its dependent universe.[3] On the contrary, sovereignty means the power to create any possible universe, including one in which significantly free agents are involved. Such a universe would owe its existence entirely to God's will, but what happens might or might not conform to God's intentions and values. God could create a world in which he determined every last detail in it, but he is not compelled to do so, and in the case of our world he did not do so.

When we say that God created the world, we mean that God exists in himself, independent of creation, and that he called the world into existence by a free and sovereign act. This means that we believe God to be ontologically other—the world being dependent on God, not God on the world. God's essence is to exist; he exists necessarily. But the world exists by grace and owes its existence to God. It would fall away into nothingness if God decided to let that happen. Thus we reject dualism—the idea of two ultimate principles, God and the world. In the ancient world Plato believed that God had to face a universe he did not create. In the modern world Whitehead has agreed. But according to the Bible all reality is dependent on God the Creator, and there are no limits to God's power except those God should decide to accept. All beings other than God have their existence from God as a gift, and whatever autonomy they possess they have also as a gift.[4]

To say that God is the sovereign Creator means that God is the ground of the world's existence and the source of all its possibilities. But he is not necessarily the puppet master who pulls all the strings. It is possible for God to make a world with some relative autonomy of its own, a world where there exist certain structures which are intelligible in their own right and finite agents with the capacity for free

---

[3]Antony Flew, *God and Philosophy* (London: Hutchinson, 1966), p. 47.
[4]A fine book about creation is Langdon Gilkey, *Maker of Heaven and Earth* (New York: Doubleday, 1959).

choice. Thus, God gives a degree of reality and power to the creation and does not retain a monopoly of power for himself. His sovereignty is not the all-determining kind, but an omnicompetent kind. God is certainly able to deal with any circumstances which might arise, and nothing can possibly defeat or destroy God. But he does not control everything that occurs. God honors the degree of relative autonomy which he grants the world.

But how can God bring his will to pass in a world where finite agents are free to resist him? He can do it because of his ability to anticipate the obstructions the creatures can throw in his way and respond to each new challenge in an effective manner. Israel may resist and rebel against God's purpose, but given time God's plan will succeed anyway. An individual may opt out of God's plan of salvation and grieve God's heart, but that cannot prevent God's kingdom from coming. It is possible to grant a sphere of significant freedom in the world without fearing that God's basic goals will be realized. Nothing can happen which God has not anticipated or cannot handle.

Before passing on to an analysis of human freedom and the sovereignty God exercises, there are three matters to comment on. First, the creation is an expression of God's purposive activity in time. God framed a purpose and then carried it out. It is important to notice not only that creation is an event and not a myth, but also that God acts temporally and not timelessly. One thing we ought not to do if we hope to make sense out of God's free agency and our own is to think of God as timeless. I will return to this later.[5]

Second, God is not independent of the world in every sense. For example, he is not like the God of Aristotle who was described as preoccupied with himself and not knowledgeable of the world. According to the Bible, God most certainly knows and cares for the world. He is, therefore, dependent on it, at least in the sense of knowing about it. God takes account of what is happening in the world and responds appropriately. Thus, in a sense, God is dependent on the world for information about the world. But God's nature is not changed because of this. Only the content of his experience of the world changes. Such

---

[5]Gordon D. Kaufman deals profoundly with God as a purposeful agent in world history in *Systematic Theology: A Historicist Perspective* (New York: Scribner's, 1968).

cognitive dependency is something God accepted when he made a significant universe outside of himself. God continues to love the world and to hate injustice, but how he expresses his love and how he reveals his holiness will vary appropriately according to the circumstances. New information flows in, and God takes account of it. On this point conventional theism has to be corrected. I will return to this later.

Third, in order to ward off the suspicion that I am a process theist, let me clarify the situation. I am sympathetic with a number of motifs in process theism. I, too, see reality as open, not closed. And I think of God as relating to events as they happen, not timelessly. But I also assert with classical theism the doctrine of creation and the ontological independence of God from the world. I hold to a dynamic theism which accepts the biblical portrayal of a God who works sequentially in a temporal process which is not an illusion.[6]

Creaturely Freedom
According to the Bible, it was not only possible for God to create a world with significantly free finite agents. God actually did exactly that. This is apparent from two central biblical assertions about human beings: (1) they are historical agents who can respond to God in love; and (2) they are sinners who have deliberately rejected God's plan for them. Neither assertion would make sense unless we posit the gift of freedom in the strong sense.

The Bible presents the creation of human beings in the image of God and talks about them as moral agents who are to have dominion over the world and respond freely to God's command (Gen 1:27-28; 2:15-17). They are like God in the fact that they reflect his own creative agency in being able to make plans and carry them out. They have the ability to transform the creation and themselves and to act self-consciously to the glory of God. It means that a personal relationship, which is the wonder of the universe, is possible between these creatures and their Maker. Human beings are able to respond (or refuse to) in love to their Creator and enter into partnership with God. By its very nature this covenant relationship cannot be coerced but is something

---

[6]Royce G. Gruenler has critiqued process theism from the perspective of classical theism. I myself am more sympathetic to it than the author is. See his *The Inexhaustible God: Biblical Faith and the Challenge of Process Theism* (Grand Rapids, Mich.: Baker, 1983).

which both parties enter into voluntarily. In the light of this possibility we must conclude that human freedom is significant and real. The response of faith and love cannot be forced. Though human freedom is limited and finite when compared with God's freedom, it is a most precious reality. The future lies open before us, and we can choose whether to make the journey with God.[7]

Creaturely freedom, of course, is not without real limits and restrictions. Our freedom comes only gradually into play in the first years of life. We are shaped to a large extent by our parents who make most of the decisions for us in the beginning. We continue to be affected by other people, as well as having an effect on them. We can lock ourselves into situations where our actual freedom is greatly diminished, or we can make decisions which expand the range of our liberty. The past has an effect on us, and we are carried along in a flow of history we cannot control. Many factors and variables enter into the decisions we make. So freedom is most definitely limited and finite. But when all is said and done, the marvel is that we are not a block of stone being wholly shaped by external factors. We are historical agents who can make a significant contribution to history and do it to God's glory.

It is surely obvious why God would make the risky decision to create beings like us. It is because of the important values which could only exist if he did so. Qualities such as love and heroism can only exist if there are creatures free to practice them. It would not mean much if an animal were programmed to love and could not do otherwise. Finite freedom is required to have love in the full sense. In a well-known passage, C. S. Lewis said: "Why then did God give them free will? Because free will, though it makes evil possible, is also the only thing that makes possible any love or goodness or joy worth having. A world of automata—of creatures that worked like machines—would hardly be worth creating."[8] People must be free to enter into that saving relationship with God which God has planned for us. We must admit that it was risky for God to take the decision to make a world like ours. I can only suppose that he believed it was a risk worth taking in view of the

---

[7]On humankind as historical see Wolfhart Pannenberg, *What Is Man?* (Philadelphia: Fortress, 1970). On humankind as capable of responding, see Hendrikus Berkhof, *Christian Faith* (Grand Rapids, Mich.: Eerdmans, 1979), chap. 25.
[8]C. S. Lewis, *Mere Christianity* (New York: Macmillan, 1952), p. 49.

benefits which could accrue. Freedom had to be created if the possibility of a personal covenant between God and creatures was to exist. Nothing less would do.[9]

According to the Bible, human beings are creatures who have rejected God's will for them and turned aside from his plan. This is another strong piece of evidence that God made them truly free. Humans are evidently not puppets on a string. They are free even to pit their wills against God's. We have actually deviated from the plan of God in creating us and set ourselves at cross-purposes to God. Obviously we are free because we are acting as a race in a way disruptive of God's will and destructive of the values God holds dear for us. It is surely not possible to believe that God secretly planned our rebelling against him. Certainly our rebellion is proof that our actions are not determined but significantly free. Though we are not dualists, we must admit that history at the present time resembles the struggle of conflicting wills, as the creature strives with God in rebellion against him. The conflict between God and finite human agents is a very real one according to the biblical narrative. We may not be able to thwart God's ultimate plan for the world, but we certainly can ruin his plan for us personally and, like the scribes, reject God's purpose for ourselves (Lk 7:30).[10]

The biblical evidence leads me then to a strong definition of freedom. It is not enough to say that a free choice is one which, while not externally compelled, is nonetheless determined by the psychological state of the agent's brain or the nature of the agent's desiring. To say that Harry stole the candy bars because he wanted them is obvious—the question is, could he have refrained from stealing them in spite of his desire? The idea of moral responsibility requires us to believe that actions are not determined either internally or externally. The Bible agrees with our intuitions about choosing and moral behaving. The love God wants from us is a love we are not compelled to give. The sin God condemns us for is a sin we did not have to commit. They are actions for which there are not prior conditions which render them certain—actions which result from the genuine choices of historical agents.

---

[9]John Hick, *Evil and the God of Love* (New York: Harper and Row, 1966), pp. 311-13.
[10]See Roger T. Forster and Paul Marston, *God's Strategy for Human History* (Wheaton, Ill.: Tyndale, 1973).

Of course, there are conditions which exist prior to our decisions and affect them, and all our actions are not free to the same extent. But the point is that we do have the capacity on occasion to perform actions which could have been otherwise and to make decisions for which alternative decisions could have been substituted. Real love implies the possibility of not sinning. It makes no sense to say that we act freely if we are in fact doing what God from eternity predestined us to do. Both reason and the Bible find no sense in that proposition.[11]

An important implication of this strong definition of freedom is that reality is to an extent open and not closed. It means that genuine novelty can appear in history which cannot be predicted even by God. If the creature has been given the ability to decide how some things will turn out, then it cannot be known infallibly ahead of time how they will turn out. It implies that the future is really open and not available to exhaustive foreknowledge even on the part of God. It is plain that the biblical doctrine of creaturely freedom requires us to reconsider the conventional view of the omniscience of God.

How was it that Augustine managed to uphold creaturely freedom as his answer to the problem of evil and not have to revise his doctrine of omniscience or omnipotence? The reason, I would venture to say, is that Augustine was not altogether coherent in this matter. It is true that he thought he could absolve God from responsibility for evil by emphasizing the fall of Adam into sin through a misuse of his freedom. But his commitment to a certain type of theism threatened his defense of the divine justice. Like Philo before him, Augustine had wedded to the biblical portrait of God certain Greek presuppositions about divine perfection, notably God's immutability. This made it impossible for Augustine to think of God's learning anything he had not eternally known or changing in response to new circumstances. He thought of God as existing beyond the realm of change and time, and knowing all things past, present and future in a timeless present. However, if history is infallibly known and certain from all eternity, then freedom is an illusion. For example, Adam could not have done otherwise than he did when he sinned. But in biblical thinking had there not been a

---

[11]I am aware that Calvinists like Donald A. Carson find that it makes sense to them. See *Divine Sovereignty and Human Responsibility* (Atlanta: John Knox, 1981), pp. 206-9.

genuine possibility for Adam to have done what was right in that instance, he would not have been a free agent at all.[12]

In saying this I stand against classical theism which has tried to argue that God can control and foresee all things in a world where humans are free. Freedom, however, can exist in this context only in a verbal sense. There is no room for the kind of freedom the Bible speaks of if there is a God who knows and/or controls all things in a timeless present. Freedom means that reality is open in a way it cannot be open for such classical theism.[13]

The Rule of God

If God created finite agents with a significant degree of freedom, it follows that God would take this into account and rule accordingly over the world. This is indeed what the Bible suggests.

The Bible presents God as the superior power who does not cling to his right to dominate but steps back to give the creatures room. God invites them to have dominion over the world and sees them try to take it over from him. He calls Israel to be his servant to show forth his character, and the nation fails again and again. When God sent his own Son, he lived out the role of a servant and did not try to push people around. God's Spirit can be grieved and quenched, and resisted. The Bible gives us the picture, not of an all-determining God, but of one who gives room to human beings and accepts the consequences, good and bad, of that policy. Even when we rebel against him, God lets us go our way. Yet he calls us back and watches for us to return (Lk 15:11-32). God surrenders the exercise of some of his power in order to gain the voluntary partnership with us he so much desires. We may speak of a voluntary self-limitation of God in the decision to create our kind of world.[14]

The kingdom of God is the key expression which Jesus used for the sovereignty of God. The Lord proclaimed the coming of the kingdom,

---

[12]See Langdon Gilkey, *Reaping the Whirlwind: A Christian Interpretation of History* (New York: Seabury, 1976), chap. 7.

[13]I agree with David R. Griffin's position in *God, Power and Evil: A Process Theodicy* (Philadelphia: Westminster Press, 1976).

[14]See Langdon Gilkey, *Message and Existence: An Introduction to Christian Theology* (New York: Seabury, 1979), chap. 5, especially pp. 91-93.

a time when God's will would be done on earth as in heaven. He looked forward, as the prophets did before him, to a historical period of peace and justice. God's rule was being savagely and effectively resisted. The kingdom was present in a mystery form, but not yet in power. Full sovereignty was something that would be established in the future after much struggle. The kingdom category demonstrates the nature of God's rule as that which allows opposition to itself and works with and around the challenges it meets.[15]

Prayer also illustrates my point. God promises to hear and answer our prayers. As James bluntly puts it: "You do not have, because you do not ask" (4:2). Prayer can change the future. Because of prayer things can be different than they would have been without it. "Ask, and it will be given you" (Mt 7:7). This must mean that God summons us into partnership with himself in running the universe. His plan is open. God actually accepts the influence of our prayers in making up his mind. Prayer proves that the future is open and not closed. It shows that future events are not predetermined and fixed. If you believe that prayer changes things, my whole position is established. If you do not believe it does, you are far from biblical religion.

The sovereignty of God, then, is not to be thought of as a blueprint of everything that will ever happen, a single pretemporal decree which freezes everything into position before history even gets started. It refers instead to the activity of God, who framed the world and is working out his saving plan in the sphere of history. The goals of the plan are unchangeable (for example, to call people into fellowship with God). But the outworking of the plan is flexible and responsive to what happens. God is constantly making decisions which bear upon the realization of his will. God responds to events in time and works every-thing together for good. But it is not a controlled situation where nothing unexpected happens and everything turns out just as God wants. It would be relatively simple to administer a world in which God could count on everything turning out as decreed. It takes a lot more

---

[15]The two most prominent theologians of the present time, Wolfhart Pannenberg and Jürgen Moltmann, both grasp firmly the sovereignty of God as coming to be effective in the future.

divine attention to work with a world where creatures are free.[16]

But is God omnipotent? Someone is bound to object that God would be finite if he did not control every detail of the world. Of course God is omnipotent. The power to create a world with free agents in it is surely omnipotent power! Only an omnipotent being, as Kierkegaard has said, would have the kind of power needed in such a project. The power of tyranny can make people obey on command, but it calls for a higher kind of power to create and work with the delicate flower of human freedom.[17]

God exercises the kind of omnipotence which is compatible with his own decision to create a world with free agents. Theists have never claimed that God could do impossible or self-contradictory things. God uses his power to sustain the kind of world he created and to promote the salvation of humankind in a noncoercive manner. Omnipotence means that God can do what he chooses to do. He could create a race of automata if he wanted to. Or he could create beings capable of engaging in free actions. His decision to do the latter is a revelation, not a denial, of his omnipotence.[18]

While my view does not deny omnipotence, properly defined, it does deny omnipotence as it has been thought of in traditional Western theology since Augustine. Even though he spoke of human freedom, Augustine was adamant in saying that God's will is always done and the creature can do nothing to prevent it. In one of his many such phrases Augustine says, "God is not truly called almighty if he cannot do whatsoever he please, or if the power of his almighty will is hindered by the will of any creature whatsoever."[19] Classical theism assumes that God's will is always and invariably done. But this is not a scriptural assumption. And it introduces enormous problems of every kind into theology and life. Such a view implies that evil is not evil because God willed it. It implies that freedom is not freedom because there are not

---

[16]Richard Swinburne, *The Existence of God* (Oxford: The Clarendon Press, 1979), chap. 10; Michael J. Langford, *Providence* (London: SCM Press, 1981).

[17]Søren Kierkegaard, *Journals* (New York: Harper and Row, 1958), p. 113.

[18]I am in complete agreement with Axel Steuer, "The Freedom of God and Human Freedom," *Scottish Journal of Theology* 36 (1983): 163-80; and Richard Swinburne, *The Coherence of Theism* (Oxford: The Clarendon Press, 1977), chap. 9.

[19]Augustine, *The Enchiridion*, chap. 96, in *Nicene and Post-Nicene Fathers*, vol. 3, ed. Philip Schaff (Grand Rapids, Mich.: Eerdmans, 1956), p. 267.

genuine alternatives. It tells us that anything we may in the future
decide has already been decided. I recognize that this belief in strong
omnipotence gives one a feeling of security, but it also communicates
a denial of the dynamic reality of the lives we are living. It mystifies me
why conservative thinkers are so reluctant to abandon the classical
framework at this point but rather continue to struggle within it.[20]

The Nature of God
If one starts exploring this subject of sovereignty and freedom one will
have to end up discussing the doctrine of God. In the last analysis the
debate in this book is about the nature of Christian theism.

The profile of God which I derive from reading the Bible is characterized by flexibility and dynamism. Our Lord is the living God who
acts and reacts on behalf of his people. He does not exist far off in
splendid isolation from the realm of time and change but relates to his
creatures and shares their lives with them. We might compare Aristotle's God to Satan in the biblical narrative in that he lives in solitary
isolation, relating to nothing and contemplating only himself. How
ironical that the aloofness of Aristotle's God should have influenced
the Christian doctrine of God and done so much damage to it. I believe
God relates to his creatures in every dimension of their lives. Far from
being a denial of God's transcendence and power, this view explains
the way in which God's power and transcendence are manifested. In a
word, God is love. He is not inactive and impassive, but constantly
involved in time and history.

The Bible is full of verses which depict God as responding sensitively
to what happens on earth. Classical theists are inclined to try and dodge
this fact by claiming that such expressions are only anthropomorphic
or childish pictures not to be taken too literally. In actual fact what they
are doing is trying to avoid what the Bible says. The Bible presents God
in a very dynamic way, but they want to overlook that fact. Take

---

[20]For example, excellent theologians like Bloesch, Erickson, Fackre and even Packer
make concessions which require them to break with strong omnipotence in Augustine
and Calvin, but they refuse to do so. I attribute this timidity to the privileged position
Calvinism enjoys in what calls itself evangelicalism. See Harry Buis, *Historic Protestantism
and Predestination* (Philadelphia: Presbyterian and Reformed, 1958).

Jeremiah 18, for example. God is compared to a potter working with clay. Because the shape was spoiled, he was thinking about starting over again. Addressing Israel, God says through Jeremiah that it is an open question what he will do with them. If they repent, there will be blessing; if they do not, he will give up on them and send judgment. This sounds very much like a dynamic God who frames his will in response to what happens in history and not at all like a God locked into timelessness and unable to change in any way.

It follows then that some fresh thinking needs to be done on the attributes of God if it is the God of the Bible we want to know. Let me offer four suggestions which are both necessary and provocative.

First, we must reject the Greek model of immutability. While God is unchangeable in essence and character, he is changeable in his knowledge and actions. A God immutable in every sense cannot be the God of revelation, responding dynamically to every fresh situation. If he were immutable in the Platonic sense, the biblical picture of an active God would be in ruins. Of course God is love; this can never change. But his love in action is continually changing in relation to his people. We praise God for his wonderful deeds which he does on our behalf. This ability to change does not mean that God is fickle or capricious. It simply means that God is able to operate within a changing history, responding to everything that happens. Praise God for his changing unchangeability![21]

Second, we must be very skeptical of the claim that God is impassible—another axiom of Platonic theology. This attribute means that God cannot experience sadness or pain or even love. Nowhere, as even H. P. Owen admits, is classical theism on thinner ice. How can we possibly say God is love and in Christ suffered for our sins if God is impassible? Owen tries his best, suggesting that God can imagine what pain must be like for the creature, but he has a hard time convincing even himself.[22] The fact is that theism was wrong to impose this singularly unhelpful notion on Christian theology, and somebody needs

---

[21] Karl Barth was on the right track in *Church Dogmatics* II/1 (Edinburgh: T. & T. Clark, 1957), pp. 490ff.
[22] H. P. Owen, *Concepts of Deity* (New York: Herder and Herder, 1971), pp. 23-25.

to say so. I appreciate some of Moltmann's efforts in this regard.[23]

Third, we ought to admit that the Greek category of timelessness, while seeming to offer some advantages to the Christian theist, is more trouble than it is worth. The Bible is content to say that God is everlasting, having neither beginning nor end. This means that he is able to be involved in time and in history. God makes plans and carries them out. God takes actions and brings effects to pass—all in temporal sequence. To think of God as timeless really threatens the whole biblical account.[24] It suggests that God cannot be an agent who works sequentially in time and even that temporal change is an illusion. If God knows history in a timeless present, then our impression that some things are past while other things are future is not really true. What happened in the year A.D. 1240 and what will happen in the year A.D. 2097 are alike present somewhere in the land of timelessness. I dislike this concept for two reasons: first, because it is meaningless; and second, because it destroys the message of the Bible.[25]

Fourth, we must rethink what we mean by God's omniscience. A very high percentage of Christians hold that God knows everything, even the future, in exhaustive detail. This means that everything you and I will ever decide to do has already been spelled out in the register of what will most certainly happen. Thus the belief that we are actually choosing between alternative courses of action is a mistake and an illusion. If God now knows that tomorrow you will select A and not B, then your belief that you will be making a genuine choice is mistaken. I agree with the traditional Calvinists that strong omniscience entails strong predestination and also with Luther who argued precise-

---

[23]Jürgen Moltmann, *The Crucified God* (London: SCM Press, 1974), chap. 6. God is not immutable in his essence in the sense that he is triune—a dynamo of love and activity. See also Moltmann's *The Trinity and the Kingdom* (San Francisco: Harper and Row, 1981).

[24]I am delighted to be able to share this conviction with an evangelical philosopher I much admire: Nicholas Wolterstorff, "God Everlasting," in *Contemporary Philosophy of Religion*, ed. Steven M. Cahn and David Shatz (New York: Oxford Univ. Press, 1982), pp. 77-98.

[25]Stephen T. Davis agrees in his *Logic and the Nature of God* (Grand Rapids, Mich.: Eerdmans, 1983), chap. 1. Ronald H. Nash is tempted to agree too in *The Concept of God* (Grand Rapids, Mich.: Zondervan, 1983), p. 83.

ly this against Erasmus.[26] Invoking timelessness as C. S. Lewis and Aquinas do is no help. If God knows eternally that A will be the selection and not B, then it is still an illusion that any genuine alternative will exist at the time of the decision. It would appear to me that actions which are infallibly foreknown or timelessly known cannot be free in the required biblical sense.[27]

But if this is so, in what sense is God omniscient? God is omniscient in the sense that he knows everything which can be known, just as God is omnipotent in the sense that he can do everything that can be done. But free actions are not entities which can be known ahead of time. They literally do not yet exist to be known. God can surmise what you will do next Friday, but cannot know it for certain because you have not done it yet.

I would appeal to the reader to try reading the biblical story with this view in mind. The problem is that readers almost never do that, even though I would argue that the storyline of the Bible almost certainly assumes it. According to the Bible, God anticipates the future in a way analogous to our own experience. God tests Abraham to see what the patriarch will do, and then says through his messenger, "Now I know that you fear God" (Gen 22:12). God threatens Ninevah with destruction, and then calls it off when they repent (Jon 3:10). I do not receive the impression from the Bible that the future is all sewn up and foreknown. The future is envisaged as a realm in which significant decisions can still be made which can change the course of history.[28]

But what about predictive prophecy? Doesn't it prove that God

---

[26]I agree with Loraine Boettner that foreknowledge entails foreordination. One must question both in order to question either. See *The Reformed Doctrine of Predestination* (Philadelphia: Presbyterian and Reformed, 1965), pp. 42-46. Luther constructed this rigorous connection in *Bondage of the Will.* See Harry J. McSorley, *Luther: Right or Wrong?* (New York: Newman Press, 1969).

[27]I agree with Nelson Pike, "Divine Omniscience and Voluntary Action" in Cahn and Shatz, *Contemporary Philosophy,* pp. 61-76.

[28]Evangelicals who have been courageous enough to make this point (some will say foolish enough) include: L. D. McCabe, *Divine Nescience of Future Contingencies* (New York: Phillips and Hunt, 1882) and *The Foreknowledge of God and Cognate Themes in Theology and Philosophy* (New York: Hitchcock and Walden, 1878); Gordon C. Olson, "The Foreknowledge of God," unpublished paper, 1941; Roy Elseth, *Did God Know? A Study of the Nature of God* (St. Paul: Calvary United Church, 1977); and Rice, *Openness.*

knows everything about the future? No, it does not. A very high percentage of prophecy can be accounted for by one of three factors: the announcement ahead of time of what God intends to do, conditional prophecies which leave the outcome open, and predictions based on God's exhaustive knowledge of the past and the present. I suggest that the crystal-ball variety of divine omniscience is not biblical in its origin, not presupposed by the biblical writers. Therefore, we should not presuppose it. We need to read the Bible more literally.

The vigorous flavor of my essay will suggest to the reader that I think it rather urgent that Christians rethink aspects of their theism. If we are going to preach the Bible and relate to people's needs effectively, then it is imperative that we highlight God's loving relativity to a changing world and diminish our commitment to the changeless divinity implied in Greek philosophy. Classical theism tried to combine these two ideals of perfection and failed to do so coherently, leaving us with a mass of unnecessary problems.[29]

In conclusion, the Bible contains many thousands of verses. I am not claiming that there are none that could be cited which might embarrass my view or any other view about the sovereignty of God and human freedom. I am only claiming that the overwhelming impression the Bible leaves us with is one of significant human freedom and dynamic divine sovereignty. God gives us room to make genuine decisions and works alongside us in the temporal process. What we are and do matters to God. God responds to us like a dancer with her partner, moving at just the right moment in perfect coordination and balance with the living person to whom she is responding. As Gordon Kaufman put it: "God's perfect responsiveness is the quality which enables him to deal with every new happening in the created order with freshness and creativity, bending it toward his ultimate objectives without violating its own integrity."[30] But if we are going to be able to think of sovereignty and freedom in this attractive and biblical way, then we will not

---

[29]I said some things along this line in an article: "The Need for a Scriptural, and Therefore a Neo-Classical Theism," in *Perspectives on Evangelical Theology*, ed. Kenneth S. Kantzer and Stanley N. Gundry (Grand Rapids, Mich.: Baker, 1979), pp. 37-42. My present views were anticipated, too, in *Grace Unlimited* (Minneapolis: Bethany Fellowship, 1975), which I edited.

[30]Kaufman, *Systematic Theology*, p. 239.

be able to avoid doing some thinking about the doctrine of God which would be in keeping with this understanding.[31]

Practical Application

Fred's Case. In my opinion a high percentage of the practical difficulties people have in this area are due to a defective theological framework. If one believes that God is immutable, omnipotent and omniscient, in the strong sense of those terms, all kinds of practical difficulties are created. Why did God will this tragedy? How can God sympathize with my struggles? How am I free if everything I will ever decide is fixed and frozen in God's timeless present or eternal decree? How does God love me if he cannot feel anything? Questions such as these can only be answered with great difficulty on the basis of conventional theism.

On the other hand, if one believes that God is a dynamic, caring agent operating in time, these difficulties do not arise. Freedom is real, and the future is open. God permits tragedies to happen which he does not will and which in fact he grieves over. What I decide is not fixed in timeless decree. God is capable of feeling gladness and sorrow, and does adjust his plan in response to changing circumstances.

Neither of the two case studies we were given present any great difficulty for my understanding of God, sovereignty and freedom. In Fred's case, he was right in the beginning to be thankful to God for placing him in North America (implied, I think) where the conditions are right for productive persons to prosper. I refer to the conditions of a Protestant attitude toward one's secular vocation and to political and economic liberty. This combination of factors has produced tremendous wealth wherever they have existed in the past two centuries, and Fred was a beneficiary of living under them. His own thrift, dedication and productivity in this context would naturally lead to prosperity. I am not certain what his belief in God's sovereign control was exactly. In my view what accounted for his prosperity was the general creative structure established by God which rewards certain kinds of behavior and penalizes other kinds. God prospered Fred, miraculously

---

[31]Nash, *Concept,* chap. 2. Ronald Nash looks at two kinds of theisms, classical and process, and sees that something in the middle is clearly needed. I have tried to express what that middle-position theism might be.

and arbitrarily, but by the way he set up the world. Fred ought to be thankful that he was born and raised in a place where his own efforts could flourish and not be squelched by factors beyond his control.

At a certain point in his life Fred became aware of the poverty of other people and places. Being a disciple of Jesus, he was troubled and concerned and wondered how he could help. It seems that he was told that poverty elsewhere was somehow due to his own prosperity in material things. Understandably he was confused and troubled and began to feel a lot of guilt. Fred's basic problem in my opinion is that he was misinformed. It is simply not true that the wealth of North America was acquired through injustice or at the expense of the poorer countries. On the contrary, North America gained its wealth because it as a culture desired material advancement and had the political-economic arrangements which are dynamically wealth-producing and without equal in human history. I think Fred probably read certain evangelical and left-oriented materials which drew him into believing in the hypothesis of Western guilt, a view first propounded by Marx and Lenin, and a theory which is very nearly the opposite of the truth. P. T. Bauer has argued for decades, effectively I think, that the poorest countries are those which had little or no contact with Western culture, while those less badly off are countries which had more extensive contacts. The sad fact is that a great number of countries in the so-called Third World have cultural-religious attitudes and political systems which impede their economic development. They blame the United States because that is easier than facing the facts. Besides, they envy the United States for being so successful in relation to themselves. My advice to Fred would be to read better-informed literature and stop torturing himself needlessly.[32]

What ought Fred to do now? First, he should acquaint himself with the facts about world poverty and its real causes. Second, he should

---

[32]See Peter T. Bauer, *Dissent on Development* (Cambridge: Harvard Univ. Press, 1976) and his famous article "Western Guilt and Third World Poverty," in *Commentary* 61 (1976): 31-38. An evangelical economist with the same view is Brian Griffiths, *Morality and the Market Place* (London: Hodder and Stoughton, 1982), chap. 5. I can only speculate that Fred was reading too much in *Sojourners* or *The Other Side* or perhaps Ronald Sider. He might even have read some article by the early Pinnock before I saw the error of my ways.

open his heart to the needy and ask what works of charity he should undertake, whether by giving or acting himself. Third, he should support the kind of liberation theology which is not linked to Marxist nonsolutions but preaches Christ as the only way to transform the religious-moral culture and which encourages freedom of enterprise in the political and economic spheres. Such a liberation praxis does hold out a little hope for improvement. The liberation theology currently in vogue offers only empty promises, and if successful, would very likely result in tyranny and socialized poverty.

Mary's Case. All Mary needs to realize is that God's will, like life itself, is dynamic and flexible. She has to dismiss the idea, drilled into her head by conventional theists, that God's will is a blueprint on which is set forth everything that will ever take place. If there were such a blueprint, of course, she wouldn't have to worry about anything— whatever will be, will be, and will be stamped with God's approval. God must have decided Mary should fail to be a doctor in his sovereign wisdom. There is no way an individual could miss a single aspect of a will that is certain and irresistible. (Even my argument against predestination was predestined!) But such a picture of the will of God is unscriptural. There is no blueprint anywhere on which it says that Mary must be a nurse and not a doctor. God's will for Mary is that she should grow in likeness to Christ and realize her fullest potential within the given situation.

Mary may have been denied entrance into medical school because she did not have the talents to succeed in medicine. Or, it may have been because the American Medical Association had seen to it that the number of candidates are kept low to protect the privileges of the profession. Or, she may have run into a male-chauvinist interviewer who decided there are too many women doctors already. Her pastor was a wise, dynamic theist who advised her not to blame God for this, but to make the best of her possibilities in nursing. He might have added that if an unjustice had been perpetrated upon her, God would look kindly on her demand for some justice. I'm glad he didn't say, "Mary, God must have wanted you to fail to get into medical school." Only determinists could be sure this was true, because for them whatever happens had to happen. Who knows, maybe down the road Mary will get a second chance to apply and succeed in becoming a doctor after all. Since reality is open, anything involving free decisions can turn out differently.

The proper stance Mary and all of us ought to have in this area of knowing God's will for our lives is one of trust. God is with us as we make our plans and move ahead. He sees a great deal more of what is going on than we can as finite creatures. We may not be able to see what good can possibly be salvaged, given some of the zigs and zags we go through in the course of the years. But we have placed ourselves in the hands of an expert who can work things together for our good and need not be anxious. God's ways are higher than our ways, and we can cast all our burdens on the Lord. Mary needs to see her life in the context of the loving purposes of God for her, and thus be liberated from worrying herself as she has been doing.[33]

---

[33]Gary Friesen is on the right track in seeing the will of God in dynamic, developing terms, but spoils the effect in my opinion by clinging to the idea of a detailed blueprint hidden from us. See *Decision Making and the Will of God: A Biblical Alternative to the Traditional View* (Portland: Multnomah Press, 1980). If only it were a more consistent alternative.

John Feinberg's Response

CLARK PINNOCK PRESENTS AN EXAMPLE OF AN INDETERMINISTIC POSI-
tion. His views can be broadly characterized as Arminian, though his
view of God certainly departs from notions typically held by Arminians.
Though I disagree with much of his essay, in what follows I shall focus
on major items of concern.

A major underlying problem of the essay is that Pinnock's understanding of and presentation of the notion of freedom begs the question. Pinnock repeatedly speaks of "true freedom," "significant freedom," and "genuine freedom" by which he means, of course, his own
contra-causal notion of freedom. He refuses to recognize any other
notion of freedom as even *possible*. Thus, he thinks the notion of causal
determinism automatically and by definition contradicts the notion of
freedom (that is the sense in which I use *impossible* in what follows).
However, such a view is question begging, since as I have shown there
is a way for determinists to speak of freedom. My intent is not to
commit the same error by claiming that only my notion of freedom is
correct or even possible, but only to note that before the evidence
favoring various notions of freedom has been assessed, one has no right
to forestall debate by refusing to admit that there is any other *possible*
notion of freedom but one's own.

Does Pinnock actually commit this logical error? Several examples will suffice to demonstrate that he does. On page 149 Pinnock offers as proof of human freedom the fact that people are able to rebel against God. Pinnock writes, "It is surely not possible to believe that God secretly planned our rebelling against him. Certainly our rebellion is proof that our actions *are not determined but significantly free*" (italics mine). This is an obvious illustration of the problem. According to Pinnock, if actions are determined (never mind that there are different forms of determinism), they cannot be *significantly* free. But what, according to Pinnock, counts as *significant* freedom? Obviously, nothing that has anything to do with causal determinism, but that just demonstrates my point; that begs the question! Further, on pages 149-50, Pinnock argues that we cannot be morally responsible for our actions unless those actions "are not determined either internally or externally" (p. 149). When God condemns us for sin, it is because we have committed "actions for which there are not prior conditions which render them certain—actions which result from the genuine choices of historical agents" (p. 149). Again, the same problem is evident. It is clear from Pinnock's discussion that if actions are determined either by something internal or external to the agent so that prior conditions render the action certain, the agent cannot have *genuine* freedom. But that begs the question, since as I have shown, it is at least possible that the determinist's notion of freedom is a *genuine* notion of freedom. Finally, in summing up his views on freedom, Pinnock argues that if God controls and foresees all things, there cannot be room for creaturely freedom. He then writes, "There is no room for the kind of freedom the Bible speaks of if there is a God who knows and/or controls all things in a timeless present" (p. 151). These claims are circular in two ways. First, it is obvious that for Pinnock causal determinism cannot be meshed with freedom, which is why he claims there cannot be freedom *and* God's control. But that is circular since it entails that the determinist's notion of freedom is impossible. Second, he assumes that the *biblical notion of freedom* is contra-causal freedom. Surely that is implicit in the claim cited. But, since the biblical writers only say that humans have freedom but do not specify what kind, why would anyone conclude that it must be contra-causal freedom unless he or she had already assumed that such is the only type of freedom there is? I am certain Pinnock does not perceive himself to be begging the question at all in his essay, but I am just as certain that since his notion is not the only possible notion of freedom, he repeatedly commits the error of arguing in a circle.

A second problem with Pinnock's discussion is its relation to Scripture. For example, Pinnock claims that in order to give us the kind of freedom we have, God voluntarily chose to self-limit the exercising of his power (p. 152). I see the claim, but I wait in vain for the biblical passage that says God did such a thing. Perhaps Pinnock thinks that the fact of human freedom is proof that God must have limited his power. But, of course, by claiming that we have freedom, one does not automatically point out what kind, nor does one prove that God has limited his power, unless, of course, one assumes that if we have freedom at all, it *must* be indeterministic. At any rate, this is just one example where specific scriptural support would have helped, but none is offered.

On the other hand, there are some places where Pinnock seems to ignore some rather key passages of Scripture. For example, on page 151 Pinnock writes, "The Bible gives us the picture, not of an all-determining God, but of one who gives room to human beings and accepts the consequences, good and bad, of that policy." Where? Certainly not in Ephesians 1:11! Pinnock later claims (p. 153) that "classical theism assumes that God's will is always and invariably done. But this is not a scriptural assumption. And it introduces enormous problems of every kind into theology and life." If by *God's will* Pinnock means his preceptive will, I agree that God's will is not always done. On the other hand, if Pinnock means (and I am certain from his overall discussion that he does) that God's decretive will is not always done, then I disagree. However, my basic point is that if Pinnock is referring to God's decree being accomplished, how can he claim that such an idea is unscriptural in view of passages such as Ephesians 1:11? Frankly, I would be delighted to see him discuss such Scriptures, but he does not.

Third, I have a fundamental problem with all indeterministic notions of freedom, and Pinnock's indeterminism does not resolve it. Pinnock claims (p. 148) that many factors and variables enter into decision making. However, it is clear that for Pinnock such factors do not decisively incline the will in one direction or another, for such an occurrence, on Pinnock's view, would eliminate freedom. On pages 149 and 150, he explicitly states that moral responsibility is ruled out if actions are determined internally or externally and that if the act is to be free, it cannot be rendered certain by any prior conditions. When all of this is taken together, I understand it to mean that while there are factors influencing a decision, none influences it to the point of determining it or rendering it certain. All of this is fairly standard Arminian/indeterminist fare, and it is surely a possible account of freedom. My problem is that I have never been able to understand how the will chooses anything if it is not decisively inclined in one direction or another. If one responds that we just choose without decisive reason, I want to know how. Do we do it randomly? Then what of this "precious" freedom? Do we do it for some unknown reason? But then it is causally determined after all. I do not find in Pinnock an explanation of how an agent comes to choose without a decisive reason for choosing one alternative over another. I only find assertions that it must be so.

Fourth, I am very concerned about Pinnock's concept of God, though space permits brief comment on only one item. Pinnock claims (see, for example, p. 146) that while God's specific plans may be thwarted by human freedom, God can be sure his general plans will not be thwarted. However, given Pinnock's contra-causal freedom, God can neither guarantee that his specific plans nor his general plans will be accomplished, for whatever it would take to bring about his plans (general or specific) would eliminate such freedom. Given contra-causal freedom, one person or groups of people must always be able to do something other than God wants and thus overturn God's plans *whether they are specific or general.*

Finally, I am disturbed over Pinnock's denial of God's foreknowledge of future events, even though I think he rightly sees the implications of contra-causal freedom for divine foreknowledge. Though much can be said about this matter, I shall comment only on Pinnock's claims that predictive prophecy does not prove divine foreknowledge of the future. Pinnock argues that such prophecy does not prove God knows everything about the future, because "a very high percentage of prophecy can be accounted for by one of three factors: the announcement ahead of time of what God intends to do, conditional prophecies which leave the outcome open, and predictions based on God's exhaustive knowledge of the past and the present" (p. 158). Let us look at each suggestion individually. As to the first, even if many prophecies are God's announcement of what he intends to do, how does that prove Pinnock's point? If God tells us what he intends to do, then will it not be done? And, if he intends to do it, why would he not *know* ahead of time what he intends to do? If what God intends to do will not be done, then what does Pinnock mean when he says God intends to do something? Does he mean that God is just expressing his wish about what might happen? If so, I find it hard to believe that when God predicted through the prophets the first advent of Christ, for example, he was only expressing what he hoped would happen. If God tells us what he intends to do, he tells us what will happen, and if he intends to do it, he knows it will happen. Pinnock's first suggestion gets him nowhere.

I have several objections to Pinnock's second suggestion. It is difficult to agree with his claim since he gives no examples of conditional prophecies which leave the outcome open. His point becomes even harder to swallow in view of all the prophecies that appear to have no conditional element. For example, where are the conditions that left matters open in regard to prophecies about the place of Christ's birth, the fact that he would be virgin born, the fact of his rejection and ultimate death? But, even in regard to prophecies which have not yet been fulfilled, where are the conditions that leave matters open? For example, are there prophecies with conditions which leave matters open as to whether there will be a second advent of Christ or a final judgment? When Pinnock claims that a large portion of prophecy is conditional and leaves it open as to what will happen, I simply have to wonder which prophecies he means.

Moreover, if the prophecies are conditional and leave open what will happen, how do they count as prophecies of the future? If the outcome is left open then how can one say the outcome is prophesied? Furthermore, my fundamental problem is knowing what it means to say prophecies are conditional, and Pinnock doesn't explain. If it means conditions must occur for the event prophesied to occur (and then the ultimate outcome from the event is left open), that makes sense. But it is no proof that God does not know beforehand either the event that will occur or the means (conditions) to its occurrence. If by conditional prophecy Pinnock means an event will occur which then sets up conditions from which any number of outcomes may occur (the outcome is open), that will not help Pinnock either. Doesn't this at least suggest that God knows some future prophesied event, the event which sets up conditions for whatever happens?

Pinnock claims that a third group of prophecies can be explained by God's exhaustive knowledge of the past and the present. Two problems confront this suggestion. First, even if it were true, would it make the future any less certain or any less known by God (things which are not supposed to be possible on Pinnock's view of freedom)? But, second, doesn't this suggestion entail essentially that the future grows out of past and present conditions? And isn't that the thesis of some of the more hard-line forms of determinism? Thus, if Pinnock is right about this third category of prophecies, he has just produced a strong argument for a strong form of determinism.

In sum, while I appreciate the fact that Pinnock has faced squarely the implications of his views on freedom for the matter of divine foreknowledge, I remain entirely unconvinced that his claims about prophecy eliminate any problems for his view that God does not know the future. Moreover, given my other concerns, I remain unconvinced in general about Pinnock's overall position.

Norman Geisler's Response

FIRST OF ALL, I AGREE WITH PINNOCK WHEN HE NOTES THAT "IN THE LAST analysis the debate in this book is about the nature of Christian theism" (p. 154). Second, he is also correct in observing that "classical theism assumes that God's will is always and invariably done" (p. 153). This is because classical theism, as held by all the great medieval and reformed theologians, accepts the attributes of God's nature which Pinnock denies, including unchangeability, simplicity, eternity, and infallibility of foreknowledge. Third, Pinnock has retained some of the elements of the classical view of God. I certainly agree with him that "God exists in himself, independent of creation, and . . . called the world into existence by a free and sovereign act" (p. 145). Fourth, I also concur with Pinnock's judgment that acceptance of any suprarational antinomy hypothesis to explain sovereignty and freedom is too high a price to pay. Fifth, I agree with his basic understanding of the nature of a free choice as self-determining, which is opposed to Feinberg's form of divine determination (causality).

Most of my differences with Pinnock spring from his rejection of the classical view of God. First of all, this explains his departure from the historically orthodox view of the infallibility (and inerrancy) of Scripture.[1] If, as Pinnock holds, the future cannot be known infallibly ahead

---

[1]See Rex A. Koivisto, "Clark Pinnock and Inerrancy: A Change in Truth Theory," *Journal of the Evangelical Theological Society* 24, no. 2 (June 1981): 139-51.

of time by God, then even the biblical predictions made by God are not infallible. Further, if God cannot know the future for sure, then even traditional Arminianism is impossible, for Arminians believe predestination is based on infallible foreknowledge of our free choice. So, in the historic sense, if Pinnock's view of God is right, then he cannot even be an Arminian!

Second, the view of God which Pinnock embraces rejects classical theism for a more neoclassical perspective in the tradition of Whitehead, Hartshorne and Ogden.[2] According to this view, God is temporal, changeable, fallible, and complex in his nature. However, once one accepts such radical changes in the classical view of God, the whole interrelated structure of historically orthodox theology collapses. It is my conviction that this is too high a price to pay for what Pinnock himself once called his "temporary flirtation with a temporal God."

Third, there are serious problems with a neoclassical view of God. If God is temporal, then he must also be spatial, since space and time are correlative. And if God is a space-time being, then he is subject to entropy (degeneration) as is the whole space-time universe. Further, if God's nature is limited to space and time, then his thoughts cannot travel any faster than the speed of light—the ultimate speed for anything in the space-time universe.[3] But if this is so, then God could not even give general direction (let alone specific providence) to the whole universe. He would not be able to comprehend the whole universe at any one moment, as neoclassical theists inconsistently claim he can. On top of all this, if God is identified with the space-time universe, then he must have had a beginning, for it can be shown scientifically that the space-time universe had a beginning.[4] Finally, if this neoclassical God had a beginning, then he is not the Creator but is really only a creature. But since Pinnock believes that God created the world from nothing, then logically he should reject this neoclassical view of God

---

[2]For a critique of neoclassical theism (process theology) see my "Process Theology," in Stanley N. Gundry, *Tensions in Contemporary Theology* (Chicago: Moody Press, 1976), pp. 237-84; and my "Process Theology and Inerrancy," in *Challenges to Inerrancy: A Theological Response*, ed. Gordon R. Lewis (Chicago: Moody Press, 1984), pp. 247-84.
[3]See Royce Gruenler, *The Inexhaustible God* (Grand Rapids, Mich.: Baker, 1983), pp. 75-76.
[4]Robert Jastrow, *God and the Astronomers* (New York: Norton, 1978), p. 14.

as well, including the attribute of temporality. If God created the whole temporal world, then God is beyond time. Conversely, if God is by nature temporal, then God did not create the whole temporal universe. He cannot create himself!

Fourth, Pinnock argues that prayer proves the future is open and not closed. But this simply confuses God's eternal vision (which is complete) with our temporal viewpoint (which is not). God has determined all things, but he has determined that prayer would be the means to accomplish some things. This in no way proves that we are not free to pray. God knew who would freely pray when he predetermined to use prayer to achieve his ends. So it is open to us to change the world by prayer, but it will not catch God by surprise when we do.

Fifth, Pinnock's contention that since God knows time then he must be temporal is confused. If this were true then one could also argue (wrongly) that since God knows creatures, then he must be a creature. Just because God knows about temporal succession does not mean he must know as temporal beings do. This is an unwarranted anthropocentrism. Furthermore, it is impossible for an independent Being, such as Pinnock claims God is, to know in a dependent way. God must know in accordance with his own Being, which even Pinnock admits is "ontologically other" than the temporal world (p. 145). Thus, God knows what temporal dependent beings know, but he does not know it the way they know it.

Sixth, the confusion in this neoclassical view of God seems to be caused by a failure to distinguish God's attributes from his activity. God's nature is above time, but his acts are in time. In short, God is eternal, but he does temporal things. Hence, God acts from eternity, but the results are in time.

Further, since actions of the eternal God are continually manifest in the temporal world, it is a false disjunction to claim that a timeless God is not productive and dynamic. His actions are perpetually productive. But an eternal God cannot be reduced to his temporal actions any more than a Creator can be reduced to his creation. Pinnock admits that God is an uncreated Creator of a world which is not uncreated. If this is so, then God can be an eternal cause of what is not eternal. Of course, God acts in time, but this no more makes his essence time-bound than creating a dependent being makes God a dependent being.

Seventh, ironically Pinnock does not avoid the very Greek dualism he disavows. The modern father of this neoclassical view, Alfred North Whitehead, admitted his view was merely an updating of Plato.[5] In view of the acknowledged Greek origin of this view, it is strange indeed for Pinnock to reject the classical view because it is Greek! This complaint is an old straw man often constructed when someone wishes to reject some aspect of orthodox theology. The time is overdue to drop the ad hominem stereotypes, caricatures and straw-men attacks on the classical orthodox view of God and to reveal the radical departure of these neoclassical views from the I AM of Moses, Jesus, Augustine, Aquinas, Calvin, Luther and Wesley. Individuals have every right to deviate substantially from the orthodox view, but they have no right to consider themselves orthodox when they do.

Eighth, there are other problems with the neoclassical view. Pinnock believes in the ultimate victory of God over evil. Yet his neoclassical view of God places strict limitations on what God can predict and accomplish. In fact, God cannot infallibly predict any future event involving free creatures. How then can Pinnock be sure God will eventually win over evil? How can it be more than a hope, or even a (Freudian) wish? As William James once said, "The world is all the richer for having a devil in it, so long as we keep our foot upon his neck."[6] But if God is not all-powerful and all-loving in the classical sense, then there is no such guarantee. One proponent admitted that the neoclassical God "has to wait with bated breath until the (human) decision is made."[7] Pinnock and all who adopt this view must hold their breath too, while all who embrace the God who knows "the end from the beginning" (Is 46:10) can breathe a deep sigh of relief.

What is at stake here is not an intramural debate over predestination and free will. In fact, the whole doctrinal structure of orthodox Christianity, whether Calvinistic or Arminian, is undergirded by these truths about the nature of the Christian God. In view of this, one is mystified that Pinnock is mystified "why conservative thinkers are so reluctant to

---

[5]See Alfred North Whitehead, *Process and Reality* (New York: Harper and Row, 1960), pp. 63, 68, 70, 129.
[6]William James, *Varieties of Religious Experience* (New York: Mentor Books, 1958), p. 55.
[7]Bernard Loomer, "A Response to David R. Griffin," *Encounter* 36, no. 4 (Autumn 1975): 365.

abandon the classical framework" (p. 154). Actually the reason is very simple: it is because to abandon classical theism is to abandon the very basis for orthodox doctrines. This ought to concern Pinnock, as well as everyone who reads this dialog.

Bruce Reichenbach's Response

APART FROM CLARK PINNOCK'S TREATMENT OF GOD'S FOREKNOWLEDGE, there is little of his theological presentation with which I disagree. He presents clearly and forthrightly the view that God's sovereignty is not to be understood on the analogy of a puppet master pulling the strings. He rightly sees that though God is unchanging in his essential nature, he is in dynamic relation with the world he created, a world that is truly open to human action and meaningful divine intervention.

As to our theological point of disagreement, it is not that he has misdefined God's omniscience. He has noted correctly that God's omniscience must be defined in a way parallel to God's omnipotence. Just as God is omnipotent in the sense that he can do everything that is not absurd or contradictory, so God is omniscient in that he can know everything that can be known. Where we differ has to do with what can be known. Pinnock contends that since future free acts cannot be known, God's ignorance of them does not count against his omniscience. But why cannot future free actions be known? He argues as follows:

1. Future free actions are events which have not yet occurred.
2. Whatever has not yet occurred cannot be known in advance.
3. Therefore free actions cannot be known in advance (p. 157).

But statement 2 is not true. The mere fact that an event has not yet occurred does not mean that the event cannot be known in advance. For example, tomorrow's eclipse of the sun has not yet occurred, yet the astronomer knows in advance that it will occur.

Pinnock might redo his argument to take account of events which we can know in advance because they follow necessarily from natural laws known to us. He might argue, for instance, as follows:

4. Future free actions are events which have not yet occurred and which do not follow necessarily from prior causal conditions or natural laws.

5. All events which have not yet occurred and which do not follow necessarily from prior causal conditions or natural laws cannot be known in advance.

6. Therefore, future free actions cannot be known in advance.

Unfortunately, however, premise 5 is also false. For example, the fact that I chose to have breakfast at home this morning does not follow necessarily from prior causal conditions or from a set of physical or natural laws, yet I could still know yesterday that this would occur, based on the evidence of my past behavioral patterns. These behavioral patterns, however, do not cause me to have breakfast at home nor provide a natural law regarding my choice of an eating place, though they provide justification for my true belief that I would eat breakfast at home.

In short, Pinnock has not established his claim that one cannot know future actions of free persons, and thus has not shown that this kind of knowledge is unavailable to God.

His other argument in support of his particular characterization of divine foreknowledge is that there is a contradiction between foreknowledge and human freedom. I have argued elsewhere in this book that this is false, that to think there is a contradiction confuses the order of causes (what brings about an event) with the order of knowledge (that upon which knowledge of the event is based). Since Pinnock does not construct his own argument to show this contradiction, I will simply refer the reader to my own discussion.

Finally—and on another topic—he characterizes God's sovereignty in terms of God's self-existence, his act of creation (both original and sustaining) and the ultimate establishment of his kingdom. God, he says, bends his created order in ways which will enable him to reach his ultimate objectives. How does he bend it, and to what degree? He rightly rejects a view of sovereignty in which God infallibly and certainly determines everything that occurs according to some eternal blueprint. Yet perhaps more could be said about that fine line between a God active in creation—a God with desires, purposes and the power to implement them—and humankind created free to cooperate with or resist God.

More specifically, the scriptural view also extends God's sovereignty to the individual in his current existence. Pinnock seems to acknowledge this when he notes that God *placed* Fred in North America (p. 159), in a country where prosperity is possible. Similarly, he suggests that God has loving purposes for Mary, who can place herself "in the hands of an expert" (p. 162). This raises the question as to the degree to which Pinnock sees God active in a sovereign or providential manner in our current lives.

Clearer specification is asking too much, you might suggest. Yet I think not, for we as Christians seek to know God's desires and purposes for our lives, and we ask him to lead us in ways consistent with that will. A discussion of this is what turns mere abstract theology into the living theology guiding our human existence.

Suggested Reading

Berkouwer, G. C. *The Providence of God*. Grand Rapids, Mich.: Eerdmans, 1972.

Boettner, Loraine. *The Reformed Doctrine of Predestination*. Philadelphia: Presbyterian and Reformed, 1965.

Boice, James M., ed. *Our Sovereign God*. Grand Rapids, Mich.: Baker, 1977.

Carson, Donald H. *Divine Sovereignty and Human Responsibility*. Atlanta: John Knox, 1981.

Davis, Stephen. *Logic and the Nature of God*. Grand Rapids, Mich.: Eerdmans, 1983.

Dennet, Daniel C. *Elbow Room: The Varieties of Free Will Worth Wanting*. Cambridge, Mass.: The MIT Press, 1985.

Erickson, Millard. *Christian Theology*, vol. 1. Grand Rapids, Mich.: Baker, 1983.

Feinberg, John. *Theologies and Evil*. Washington, D.C.: University Press of America, 1979.

Flew, Antony. *God and Philosophy*. London: Hutchinson, 1966.

Flew, Antony and MacIntyre, Alasdair, eds. *New Essays in Philosophical Theology*. New York: Macmillan, 1955.

Forster, Roger and Marston, V. Paul. *God's Strategy in Human History*. Wheaton, Ill.: Tyndale House, 1973.

Friesen, Gary. *Decision Making and the Will of God: A Biblical Alternative to the Traditional View*. Portland: Multnomah Press, 1980.

Geach, Peter. *Providence and Evil*. Cambridge: At the University Press, 1977.

Geisler, Norman. *The Roots of Evil*. Grand Rapids, Mich.: Zondervan, 1978.

Griffin, David. *God, Power, and Evil: A Process Theodicy*. Philadelphia: Westminster, 1976.

Gruenler, Royce. *The Inexhaustible God: Biblical Faith and the Challenge of Process Theism*. Grand Rapids, Mich.: Baker, 1983.

Hartshorne, Charles. *Omnipotence and Other Theological Mistakes*. Albany: State University of New York, 1984.

Hasker, William. *Metaphysics*. Downers Grove, Ill.: InterVarsity Press, 1983.

Hick, John. *Evil and the God of Love*. New York: Harper and Row, 1966.

Hook, Sidney, ed. *Determinism and Freedom*. New York: Collier Books, 1958.

Kenny, Anthony. *The God of the Philosophers*. Oxford: The Clarendon Press, 1979.

Langford, Michael. *Providence*. London: SCM Press, 1981.

Lucas, J. R. *Freedom and Grace*. London: SPCK, 1976.

McCabe, L.D. *Divine Nescience of Future Contingencies*. New York: Phillips and Hunt, 1982.

Nash, Ronald. *The Concept of God*. Grand Rapids, Mich.: Zondervan, 1983.

O'Conner, D. J. *Free Will*. London: Macmillan, 1972.

Packer, J. I. *Evangelism and the Sovereignty of God*. Downers Grove, Ill.: InterVarsity Press, 1961.

Pike, Nelson. *God and Timelessness*. New York: Schocken Books, 1970.
Pinnock, Clark, ed. *Grace Unlimited*. Minneapolis: Bethany Fellowship, 1975.
Plantinga, Alvin. *God, Freedom and Evil*. Grand Rapids, Mich.: Eerdmans, 1974.
Reichenbach, Bruce. *Evil and a Good God*. New York: Fordham Press, 1982.
Rice, Richard. *The Openness of God: The Relationship of Divine Foreknowledge and Human Free Will*. Minneapolis: Bethany House, 1985.
Swinburne, Richard. *The Coherence of Theism*. Oxford: The Clarendon Press, 1977.
_____ . *The Existence of God*. Oxford: The Clarendon Press, 1979.
Van Inwagen, Peter. *An Essay on Free Will*. Oxford: The Clarendon Press, 1983.

Contributors

David Basinger is presently associate professor of philosophy at Roberts Wesleyan College in Rochester, Minnesota. He earned the M.A. and Ph.D. in philosophy from the University of Nebraska. He has also contributed articles to numerous journals and magazines and has coauthored with his brother, Randall, a new book on miracles.

Randall Basinger now serves as associate professor of philosophy at Messiah College in Grantham, Pennsylvania. At Trinity Evangelical Divinity School he earned an M.A. in philosophy of religion, and he received a Ph.D. in religion from Northwestern University. He has written several articles in various journals and magazines and has coauthored with his brother, David, a new book on miracles.

John S. Feinberg is associate professor of Biblical and Systematic Theology at Trinity Evangelical Divinity School in Deerfield, Illinois. He is a graduate of the University of California, Los Angeles (B.A.), Talbot Theological Seminary (M.Div.), Trinity Evangelical Divinity School (Th.M.) and the University of Chicago (M.A., Ph.D.). He has contributed to numerous theological journals and various anthologies and has written *Theologies and Evil.*

Norman L. Geisler is author or coauthor of over twenty books, including *Introduction to Philosophy, Philosophy of Religion, Miracles and Modern Thought, The Roots of Evil* and *Christian Apologetics.* He earned a B.A. and M.A. from Wheaton College, a Th.B. from William Tyndale College and a Ph.D. (in philosophy) from Loyola University. He has served as chairman of the Philosophy of Religion Department at Trinity Evangelical Divinity School and now is professor of theology at Dallas Theological Seminary.

Clark H. Pinnock is presently professor of theology at McMaster Divinity College in Hamilton, Ontario. Prior to this he taught at Regent College, Trinity Evangelical Divinity School, New Orleans Baptist Theological Seminary, and the University of Manchester from which he earned his doctorate in New Testament studies. He is the author of several books, including *Biblical Revelation, Reason Enough* and *The Scripture Principle.* He was once a Calvinist.

Bruce R. Reichenbach is professor of philosophy at Augsburg College in Minneapolis. He completed his undergraduate work at Wheaton College and his doctoral work at Northwestern University. He has held visiting professorships at Morija Theological Seminary in Lesotho, Africa, and Juniata College. In addition to articles in various journals and periodicals, he has published *The Cosmological Argument: A Reassessment, Is Man the Phoenix? A Study of Immortality* and *Evil and a Good God.*